Free limited time bonus

Stop for a moment. We have a free bonus set up for you. The problem is this: we forget 90% of everything that we read after 7 days. Crazy fact, right? Here's the solution: we've created a printable, 1-page pdf summary for this book that you're reading now. All you have to do to get your free pdf summary is to go to the following website: **https://livetolearn.lpages.co/enthrallinghistory/**

Once you do, it will be intuitive. Enjoy, and thank you!

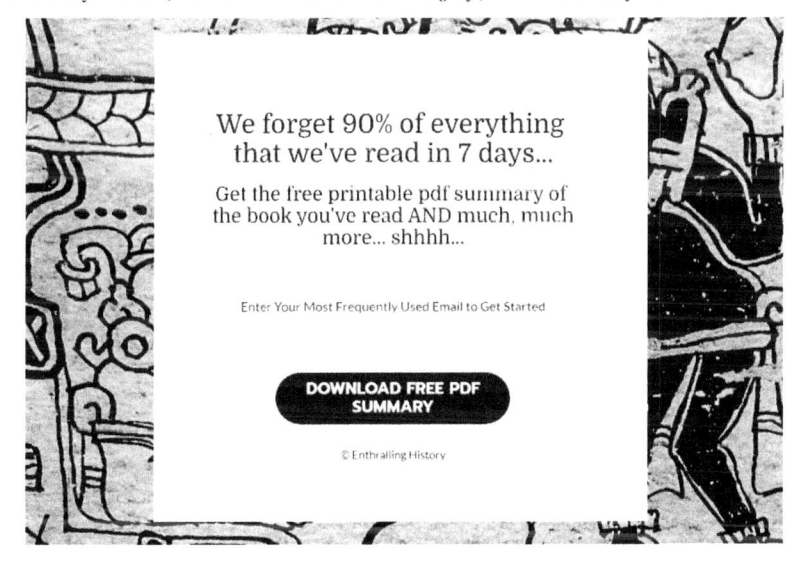

Table of Contents

INTRODUCTION 1
PART ONE: NORTH AMERICA COLONIZATION (1492-1776) 3
CHAPTER 1: EXPLORATION AND FIRST SETTLEMENTS 4
CHAPTER 2: THE THIRTEEN COLONIES 12
CHAPTER 3: THE FRENCH AND INDIAN WAR 16
CHAPTER 4: CAUSES FOR REVOLUTION 20
PART TWO: THE UNITED STATES ARE BORN (1776-1861) 25
CHAPTER 5: THE AMERICAN REVOLUTION 26
CHAPTER 6: THE CONSTITUTION AND THE BILL OF RIGHTS 36
CHAPTER 7: THE LOUISIANA PURCHASE AND THE WAR OF 1812 44
CHAPTER 8: EXPANSION IN THE WEST AND SOUTH 51
CHAPTER 9: THE MEXICAN-AMERICAN WAR, THE OREGON TREATY, AND THE GOLD RUSH 60
PART THREE: THE CIVIL WAR AND THE RECONSTRUCTION (1861-1877) 69
CHAPTER 10: WHAT CAUSED THE CIVIL WAR? 70
CHAPTER 11: KEY BATTLES AND CAMPAIGNS OF THE CIVIL WAR 74
CHAPTER 12: SLAVERY, EMANCIPATION, AND THE AFTERMATH 87
CHAPTER 13: THE RECONSTRUCTION (1865-1877) 92
PART FOUR: FROM RECONSTRUCTION TO WWI (1877-1917) 97

CHAPTER 14: FROM RECONSTRUCTION TO EXPANSION 98
CHAPTER 15: THE PROGRESSIVE ERA 104
CHAPTER 16: THE FATE OF THE NATIVE AMERICANS................... 111
CHAPTER 17: POLITICAL AND ECONOMIC CHANGES..................... 120
PART FIVE: WWI, GREAT DEPRESSION, AND WWII (1914-1945) ... 131
CHAPTER 18: WORLD WAR I AND THE ROARING '20S 133
CHAPTER 19: THE GREAT DEPRESSION AND THE NEW DEAL 140
CHAPTER 20: WWII: AMERICA BECOMES A SUPERPOWER 146
PART SIX: THE COLD WAR AND THE SPACE RACE BEGIN
(1945-1969) 159
CHAPTER 21: THE TRUMAN YEARS: THE COLD WAR BEGINS 160
CHAPTER 22: THE IKE YEARS: COUP D'ÉTATS AND CIVIL
RIGHTS.. 167
CHAPTER 23: THE KENNEDYS AND THE '60S: DREAM UP
A BETTER WORLD 176
PART SEVEN: DÉTENTE AND THE END OF THE COLD WAR
(1968-1992) 189
CHAPTER 24: THE NIXON-FORD YEARS: DÉTENTE AND
ECONOMIC CHANGES 190
CHAPTER 25: JIMMY CARTER: THE END OF DÉTENTE.................. 197
CHAPTER 26: REAGAN AND REAGANOMICS 203
CHAPTER 27: GEORGE H. W. BUSH: THE END OF THE COLD
WAR 211
PART EIGHT: FROM CLINTON TO TRUMP (1992-2021).................... 218
CHAPTER 28: THE CLINTON YEARS: THE SWIFT AND
SCANDALOUS '90S 219
CHAPTER 29: THE GEORGE W. BUSH YEARS: 9/11 AND THE
WAR ON TERROR 227
CHAPTER 30: BARACK OBAMA: THE FIRST BLACK
PRESIDENT.. 233
CHAPTER 31: DONALD TRUMP: A CONTROVERSIAL
PRESIDENT.. 240
CONCLUSION: LOOKING FORWARD... 248
HERE'S ANOTHER BOOK BY ENTHRALLING HISTORY
THAT YOU MIGHT LIKE... 249
FREE LIMITED TIME BONUS 250
SOURCES.. 251

American History

An Enthralling Overview of Major Events that Shaped the United States of America

© Copyright 2023 - All rights reserved.

The content contained within this book may not be reproduced, duplicated, or transmitted without direct written permission from the author or the publisher.

Under no circumstances will any blame or legal responsibility be held against the publisher, or author, for any damages, reparation, or monetary loss due to the information contained within this book, either directly or indirectly.

Legal Notice:

This book is copyright protected. It is only for personal use. You cannot amend, distribute, sell, use, quote, or paraphrase any part, or the content within this book, without the consent of the author or publisher.

Disclaimer Notice:

Please note the information contained within this document is for educational and entertainment purposes only. All effort has been executed to present accurate, up-to-date, reliable, and complete information. No warranties of any kind are declared or implied. Readers acknowledge that the author is not engaging in the rendering of legal, financial, medical, or professional advice. The content within this book has been derived from various sources. Please consult a licensed professional before attempting any techniques outlined in this book.

By reading this document, the reader agrees that under no circumstances is the author responsible for any losses, direct or indirect, that are incurred as a result of the use of the information contained within this document, including, but not limited to, errors, omissions, or inaccuracies.

Introduction

The United States is, without a doubt, one of the world's superpowers. It has played a significant role in international politics and has been an example that other nations have looked up to for many years.

It's almost impossible to imagine that, once upon a time, America was nothing but a handful of colonies settled by people trying to carve out a life from nothing in the unfamiliar lands of North America. This powerful nation was colonized by Europeans and has a long, complicated, rich, and often bloody history dating back centuries.

So, how did America *become* America? How did it gain such power? And how did it become a leader in the global world? This book answers all those questions and more.

For those looking for a basic introduction to American history, from its earliest colonial roots to the present day, this guide is the perfect start. This book provides a comprehensive and simple overview of some of the most critical moments and events in American history and talks about how it developed from a colony into one of the biggest and most powerful nations in the world. This topic is massive, so this will not be an all-encompassing, in-depth book on the full history of the United States. Instead, we will be giving the broad strokes, leaving you with a better understanding of how the nation evolved over time.

Turn the page to learn about America, and discover for yourself which part of American history fascinates you the most.

PART ONE: North America Colonization (1492–1776)

Chapter 1: Exploration and First Settlements

Christopher Columbus

The man commonly associated and credited with "discovering" America is Christopher Columbus. Today, the United States continues to celebrate the famous explorer with a federal holiday held on the second Monday in October. The date is meant to celebrate the moment Columbus arrived in the Americas in 1492.

However, as we all know, Columbus did not discover a brand-new country or continent. In fact, the Americas had already been inhabited by Native Americans for hundreds of years. They were descendants of hunter-gatherers who made their way to the continent tens of thousands of years ago.

Christopher Columbus likely would have been surprised to discover that he wasn't even the first European to land in the Americas. One thousand years before his arrival, Vikings had made their way to what is present-day Canada.

But in 1492, when Columbus excitedly set foot on American soil, neither he nor the people back in Europe knew this. His discovery opened the door for Europeans to begin migrating en masse to this new land.

When Columbus set sail from Spain, his goal was to find a shortcut to the East Indies. King Ferdinand and Queen Isabella of

Spain agreed to fund his voyage, and in 1492, he set off with dreams of finding the perfect spice route.

Christopher Columbus.
https://en.wikipedia.org/wiki/File:Portrait_of_a_Man,_Said_to_be_Christopher_Columbus.jpg

He ended up in The Bahamas instead, although he believed he had found India. Columbus continued his explorations and found Cuba and eventually Hispaniola. When Columbus and his men encountered natives, it created friction and problems. Columbus's arrival would be the start of the ongoing conflict between settlers and the Native Americans. The Europeans also brought a host of diseases and illnesses with them, such as smallpox, influenza, and typhus, just to name a few. These diseases had a devastating impact on the indigenous population, as they easily succumbed to these diseases since they had no built-up immunity.

Between 1492 and 1504, Columbus made four trips to the Americas. Each voyage resulted in new discoveries. And each discovery inevitably led to more violence and bloodshed.

The arrival of the explorers was the beginning of the end of life as the Native Americans knew it. Subjected to foreign diseases and unimaginable brutality and violence at the hands of the colonists, they were treated as less than human. Before the colonists arrived in

North America, Native Americans already had a way of living. They had communities with diverse cultures and ethnicities.

When the Europeans first landed in what would become the United States, their survival in the harsh, unfamiliar terrain depended largely on the generosity and help of the Native Americans. However, that generosity was often not reciprocated, and as colonists became more familiar with and settled in their new land, they turned on the very people who had helped them. Native Americans were pushed out of their land, often through force and violence. Both Native Americans and settlers committed terrible atrocities during this tense period of history.

Spanish Expeditions

As news of Columbus's discoveries spread across Europe, a series of expeditions quickly began, with kingdoms clamoring to expand their domains.

Several years after Columbus's death, King Ferdinand asked Juan Ponce de León to search for more land. He eventually discovered modern-day Florida and a passage through the Florida Keys to the Gulf of Mexico.

Explorers continued to travel to the New World as the years passed. They mainly focused on exploring Central and South America and the Caribbean. But the 16th century also saw an influx of Spanish explorers conquering parts of North America and establishing settlements on the land.

One of the better-known explorers was Francisco Vázquez de Coronado. Coronado was the governor of Nueva Galicia, a province in New Spain (present-day Mexico). He was also a conquistador. Coronado had heard stories of the Seven Golden Cities in the southwestern US and was determined to find them.

He put together an expedition, in which he invested heavily with his own money, and set off in 1540, traveling up the western coast of Mexico. He and his men ended up in the southwestern US. For the next two years, he explored the land between Mexico and Kansas. Although Coronado was the first to find Kansas, he was not the first Spaniard to venture deep into the US, as Hernando de Soto traveled as far as Arkansas, becoming the first documented European to cross the Mississippi River.

Coronado never found the treasure he was seeking, though his expedition did lead to the discoveries of the Colorado River and the Grand Canyon. However, for all intents and purposes, his expedition had been a failure. When he returned to New Spain, charges were brought against him for his conduct on the expedition against the Native Americans. He was eventually cleared of the charges and resumed his position as governor. He stayed in Mexico City until his death in 1554.

In time, other European countries began to also look toward North America.

Jacques Cartier

When Jacques Cartier, the famous French explorer, set out from France, it was hoped that he would have great success in discovering what Columbus had set out to do all those years ago. King Francis I of France wanted Cartier to find the elusive Northwest Passage: the westward route that would lead directly to Asia.

In April 1534, Cartier set out with a crew of sixty one men and two ships, intent on discovering the Northwest Passage. Instead of a route to Asia, he stumbled upon North America and explored the coast of the St Lawrence River. He ended up discovering the Gulf of St. Lawrence, the west coast of Newfoundland, and Prince Edward Island.

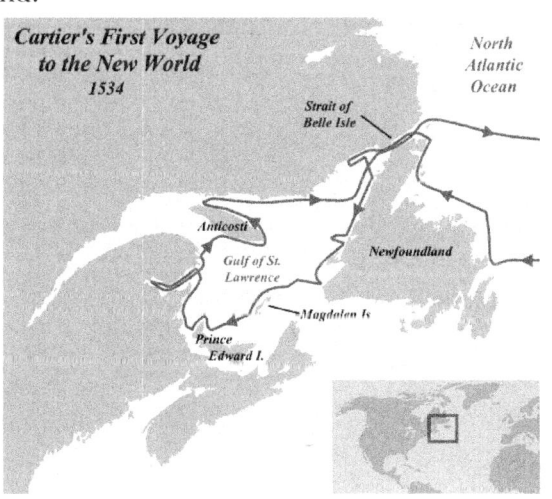

Cartier's first voyage.
Jon Platek, CC BY-SA 3.0 <https://creativecommons.org/licenses/by-sa/3.0>, via Wikimedia Commons; https://commons.wikimedia.org/wiki/File:Cartier_First_Voyage_Map_1.png

When Cartier returned to France after the first expedition, he brought two Native Americans with him that he had captured. For Cartier's next expedition, King Francis I gave him 110 crew members and an additional ship. When they reached North America, Cartier used the captive Native Americans as guides to further explore the St. Lawrence River. The explorations led them to Quebec, where a base camp was established.

Tensions started to rise with the Iroquois. On top of this, many of Cartier's crew became sick. When spring came, Cartier once again returned to France. This time, he went back with Iroquois chiefs who had been taken by force.

Cartier's final expedition took place in 1541. King Francis asked Jean-François de Roberval to lead the charge this time. He was tasked with building a permanent colony in the lands discovered by Cartier.

Cartier left a few months before Roberval. While in Quebec, he found what he believed were precious gems and gold. He immediately headed back to France, only to discover that his treasure was not treasure at all. King Francis must have been displeased by his behavior because he did not send him out for any more expeditions.

On September 1st, 1557, Cartier died, but he left behind an enormous legacy. The lands he claimed on behalf of France would go on to form part of what is present-day Canada. He is also the man who gave Canada its name; it is based on the Huron-Iroquois word *kanata*, which means village.

Roberval gave up on the idea of establishing a permanent colony. The French would not turn their attention back to these lands for over fifty years.

English Explorations and Settlements

By the 16th century, the English had already begun expanding their influence in places like Africa and Asia. Like France and Spain, England was also keen on finding a shortcut to Asia, a continent filled with riches and spices.

Henry Hudson

In 1607, English explorer Henry Hudson was hired to find a route to Asia through the Arctic Ocean called the Northwest

Passage. His first two attempts were unsuccessful due to ice. On his third voyage, which took place in 1609 and was sponsored by the Dutch, he chose to go a different route.

He ended up on the Atlantic coast and sailed on a river initially called the North River. This would later become known as the Hudson River. On September 11th, his ship sailed into Upper New York Bay. By the end of September, he decided to return to Europe. His mission to find the Northwest Passage had been unsuccessful.

He regrouped and attempted another voyage the following year. The voyage would be his last one, but it would also be one of his most memorable. On August 2nd, he and his men sailed into Hudson Bay. They believed they had found the Pacific Ocean at last, but Hudson eventually realized he had not found the Northwest Passage after all. The winter months were harsh, and the expedition was unsuccessful.

When Hudson and his crew eventually headed back to England, tensions continued to mount until the crew turned on Hudson and his son. They, along with some other men suffering from scurvy, were set adrift in the Hudson Bay on a lifeboat with scant supplies.

The world never heard from them again.

Hudson's voyages provided the foundation needed to establish Dutch colonies along the Hudson River Valley. He also opened the door for the English to claim land in Canada. Like Jacques Cartier, he left behind an enduring legacy.

Other Explorers

Once the door was opened to the New World, many explorers, like John Cabot, Sir Walter Raleigh, Martin Frobisher, and John Davis, began to embark on expeditions of their own.

John Cabot was one of the earliest explorers, setting sail not long after Columbus. Although he was Italian (his real name was Giovanni Caboto), he moved to England sometime in his late thirties and carried out explorations commissioned by King Henry VII. He felt certain there was a better way of reaching Asia.

Cabot arrived in North America. Historians believe he landed in the Newfoundland or Cape Breton area. After exploring the area, he claimed the land for the English and returned to England, excited at his discovery.

His second voyage ended in catastrophe when the ships were caught in a storm. Cabot's exact fate remains unknown, but it's believed he likely died at sea.

Sir Walter Raleigh was a later English explorer. He set out on his expedition in 1587 (almost one hundred years after Cabot had set sail). Raleigh explored the territory from Florida to North Carolina, naming it Virginia after the Virgin Queen, Elizabeth I. He also set out to find the legendary El Dorado but instead discovered tobacco and potatoes. Raleigh introduced these two products to Britain.

Although Raleigh led an impressive life filled with adventure, he was eventually charged with treason by King James I and beheaded.

Each expedition led to the discovery of another part of North America, eventually shaping it into the continent we know today.

Roanoke – The "Lost Colony"

The earliest attempt at establishing a proper and permanent colony in North America was known as Roanoke Colony. Situated off the coast of present-day North Carolina, this English colony was founded in 1585 by Raleigh. The colony was a failure, but Raleigh attempted the endeavor again a few years later, in 1587.

A small group of 115 settlers arrived on the island, intent on creating a permanent English outpost. However, they faced many hardships. Namely, they didn't have enough supplies, they had poor harvests, and they had a difficult time adjusting to the land.

John White, who was made governor of the colony, returned to England the same year to stock up on supplies. He left his wife, daughter, and granddaughter (the first English child born in the New World) behind on the island.

When White arrived in England, the country was engaged in a naval war with Spain. Queen Elizabeth I stated the priority was for all ships to fight against the Spanish Armada. White wouldn't be able to return to Roanoke until August 1590. When he did, he found that all traces of the colony had vanished. One lone clue was left behind carved into a post: the word "Croatoan."

To this day, nobody knows what happened to the colony or its inhabitants. Some speculate that they were killed by a tribe of Native Americans from an island called Croatoan, while others believe that when John didn't return, they tried to sail back to England and were lost at sea. It is also possible they went to Croatoan Island. However, nobody knows for sure what happened to the "Lost Colony."

Chapter 2: The Thirteen Colonies

What we know as the present-day United States, a massive country boasting fifty states, initially started off as thirteen British colonies grouped together to form British America.

In the early 17th century, the colonies began to be established by Queen Elizabeth, who was keen on growing the British Empire and who wanted to keep pace with Spain.

Some of these colonies had already been around since the early 17th century. Each had a specific history of its own and was founded for a wide range of reasons, such as overpopulation in Europe, more religious freedom, and business ventures.

During the 17th century, most European countries were competing with one another for power and wealth. Wealth was associated with trade, resulting in trading companies running a mad race to get colonies. The hope was that colonies in America would allow England to establish trading ports along the coast, which would lead to jobs and money. Colonists also hoped they would find precious minerals, such as gold.

Pilgrims and Puritans also sought to settle in the New World. About one hundred people sailed on the *Mayflower* to find a new life. Many of those on board were Pilgrims who wanted to escape religious persecution in England and separate from the Church of

England.

This group eventually arrived in Plymouth, Massachusetts, in 1620. The people set up trading posts in Maine and Cape Cod and received the freedom to worship as they wished. Like the other colonists, they also ran into difficulties with the Native Americans. However, they maintained a better relationship with them than other colonists.

A decade later, Puritans, who were non-separatists but still wished to change the practices of the Church of England, also migrated to the New World. They established the Massachusetts Bay Colony. The Puritans were pious people looking for economic benefits in a new land. They were also very literate and were known for writing sermons and poetry.

The Puritans founded Harvard in 1636. The university was initially established as a Congregationalist institution designed to train ministers. Over the centuries, it evolved to become what it is today, one of the most well-known and respected universities in the world.

The Puritans also founded a printing press and emphasized the importance of education. Their beliefs and influence eventually led to the American school system.

Overview of the Colonies

Many of the Thirteen Colonies were named after British royals or notable figures (for instance, Pennsylvania was named after William Penn's father) and are typically divided into three regions:

- The Middle Colonies
    - Delaware
    - New York (this colony was originally part of a Dutch colony and was called New Netherland)
    - New Jersey
    - Pennsylvania
- The Southern Colonies
    - Maryland
    - Georgia (named after King George II)
    - North Carolina
    - South Carolina (both are named after King Charles I)

- Virginia (named after the Virgin Queen, Elizabeth I)
- The New England Colonies.
  - Massachusetts Bay
  - Connecticut
  - New Hampshire
  - Rhode Island

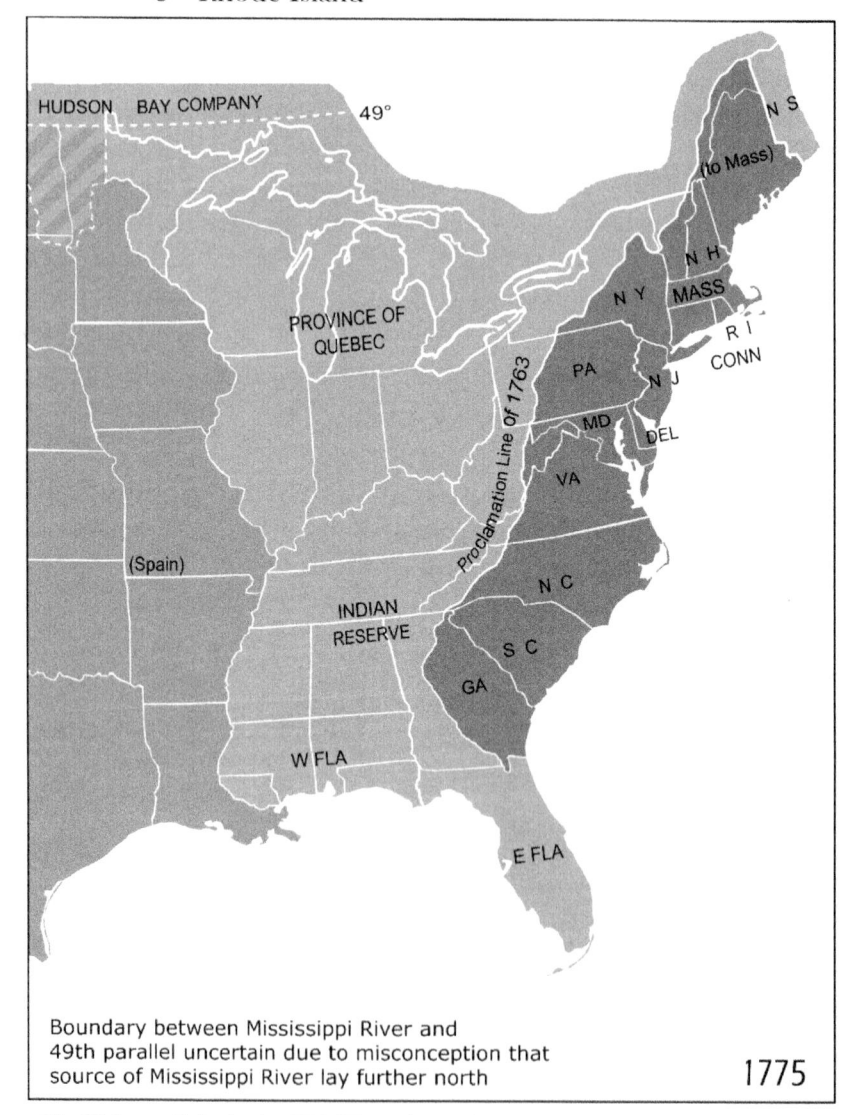

The Thirteen Colonies in 1775. The colonies fluctuated over the years, though; their borders weren't always so well established.
https://commons.wikimedia.org/wiki/File:Map_of_territorial_growth_1775.svg

Life in the colonies was extremely difficult, and conditions were often very harsh and primitive, especially during the winter months. Things got better as time passed, but Jamestown, the first permanent English settlement in North America (and the first permanent settlement in what would become the United States), was established in what would become Virginia in 1607. The colony had a very rough start. The winter of 1609/10 was called the Starving Time. There were five hundred people in the colony at the start of winter; by the end, there were only sixty-one. The settlers had to resort to cannibalism to stay alive.

It took nearly a decade for the colonists to start doing well in Jamestown, which was mostly due to growing and trading tobacco. As tobacco plantations spread and began to thrive, the colonists began to bring in slaves to work the land. The first enslaved Africans arrived in 1619.

New York was a melting pot as far back as the 17th century. Originally called New Netherland, it was established by the Dutch in 1614. The Dutch and the English had been embroiled in several wars with each other and were enjoying a truce when King Charles II gave the colony to the duke of York, his brother.

The duke of York sent Colonel Richard Nicolls to go to America and seize the colony. Armed with warships and soldiers, he did as asked and sailed into New Amsterdam (present-day New York City) in the spring of 1664 and demanded the colony's surrender. Unable to rally support from the people because of their dislike of him, Peter Stuyvesant, the Dutch governor, surrendered to the English.

Most of the population who were already settled there, including Germans, Scandinavians, and Belgians, stayed put. The people were quickly absorbed by the English, and the name of the colony was changed to New York. From its very inception, New York was one of the most diverse colonies, eventually becoming one of the most multicultural cities in the world.

The colonies in North America remained a part of the British Empire for almost 170 years. Eventually, though, the Founding Fathers broke away from the British Empire. The Thirteen Colonies became a new nation called the United States of America.

Chapter 3: The French and Indian War

French and Indian War (1754-1763)

The continued struggle and tension between France and Great Britain eventually escalated into another war in 1754. The French and Indian War is viewed as the North American theater of the Seven Years' War, which began later in 1756.

What caused the war? When France expanded its territory into the Ohio River Valley in North America during the early 1750s, it conflicted with some of the territory claimed by the British. There were also disputes over waterways, trading, and religious differences. In 1754, the royal governor in Virginia sent a group of men from the Virginia Regiment to secure the Forks of Ohio.

European colonies in North America in 1750.
Pinpin, CC BY-SA 3.0 <https://creativecommons.org/licenses/by-sa/3.0>, via Wikimedia Commons; https://commons.wikimedia.org/wiki/File:Nouvelle-France_map-en.svg

When the Virginians arrived, they discovered the French had already started to build Fort Duquesne in what is present-day Pittsburgh, Pennsylvania. Twenty-one-year-old George Washington headed the Virginian expedition to the area; he decided to go on the offensive. Things escalated from there, leading to the Battle of Jumonville Glen.

Also known as the Jumonville affair, this battle was the official start of the French and Indian War. It was also significant in that this was Washington's first armed conflict.

Before the battle broke out, Washington had arrived at Great Meadows in May; it was roughly seven miles (eleven kilometers) away from where the French set up camp. Fearful of an imminent attack, Washington struck the first blow by leading a group of soldiers to the hiding spot of the French.

The French, who were led by Joseph Coulon de Villiers de Jumonville, were decimated. However, it turns out the French were not seeking military action; rather, they were carrying a message to Washington to evacuate the area.

Jumonville was killed, as were most of his men. It's unclear what exactly happened in the battle. According to most accounts, the Native Americans aiding Washington killed and scalped Jumonville. This unexpected attack opened the floodgates for other natives to do the same, and in short order, nine French soldiers were scalped before Washington could do anything.

One soldier managed to escape, and he recounted what happened when he returned to the fort. The incensed French declared Washington to be a war criminal, leading to the Battle of Fort Necessity. That particular battle ended with Washington surrendering; it was the one and only time he would do so in his career.

Role of the Native Americans in the War

Many Native American tribes got involved in the war, but they didn't all pick the same side. The Shawnee, Seneca, Kickapoo, Sandusky, and Wea tribes allied with the French. On the British-American side were the Mohawk, Montauk, Cherokee, Cayuga, Seneca, Chickasaw, Creek, Onondaga, and Tuscarora.

The Native Americans who allied with the French did so because they were getting tired of how much control Britain was exerting on their lands and how much the colonists had already taken from them. They were increasingly being pushed out, and they hoped that if the French defeated the British, this would stop.

The Native American tribes that sided with Britain did so for much the same reason. They hoped that by giving the British support, they would be able to stop the colonists from further encroaching on their lands. The priority for the natives was to keep their tribal lands safe and in their hands.

Two years after the French and Indian War began, war erupted in Europe between France and England, triggering the beginning of the Seven Years' War.

The French were woefully outnumbered by the British, who had over two million settlers in the colonies at the start of the war. The French only had around 60,000 settlers. This made the French particularly dependent on the natives who joined forces with them.

While many in Europe saw America as another theater of the conflict, for the North American settlers, it became their own war that had nothing to do with Europe.

The war in Europe dragged on for seven years. The French and Indian War and the Seven Years' War formally came to an end after the Treaty of Paris was signed in February 1763. Under the treaty, a number of trades took place. France gave Britain its territories east of the Mississippi River. Spain handed over Florida to the British. France was allowed to keep some Canadian islands, while Spain took Louisiana from them.

Even after the war finally ended, territorial disputes continued, especially among the Native Americans, who wanted to get some of their lands back.

Impact of the War on the Colonies

The French and Indian War would become one of the catalysts for the American Revolution. The American colonists were unhappy that they were being made to shoulder the costs of the war, especially when they had no real representation in British Parliament. This created a deep divide between the colonies and the empire of Great Britain. However, the war had also drained Britain of money and resources, which it hoped to recoup from the colonies.

Immediately after the war, there was a sense of unity, purpose, and a feeling of victory amongst the colonists. They had fought in a significant war and came out as victors. However, the sense of euphoria was short-lived, as Britain began to pressure them. The colonists were suddenly feeling resentful and questioning what purpose they served and why they were doing what they were doing.

These feelings of discontent would eventually boil over into a revolution.

Chapter 4: Causes for Revolution

The American Revolution did not happen overnight.

Tensions between the Thirteen Colonies and the British Empire simmered for many years before violent conflicts broke out. Life in the colonies was far from ideal and could often be harsh and difficult. But the colonists had made things work. They prospered, and as time passed and due to certain factors, they simply had enough of the British.

Although the French and Indian War did not directly cause the American Revolutionary War, the consequences of the war triggered a chain of events culminating in the eruption of the revolution. The global conflict had ended in a victory for Britain. The British secured their authority along the Atlantic coast and brought new territories under the Crown's control. However, it would come at a high cost, as it would be the beginning of the end of Britain's control over the region.

In order to recoup the expenses incurred during the war and the many other wars fought in Europe, the Crown decided to impose taxes on the colonies. Less than two years after the war ended, the Crown passed the Stamp Act. The colonists now had to pay taxes on stamped papers, which included legal documents, newspapers, and even playing cards! The colonists fought back against the act, and it was repealed in 1766. However, it wouldn't be the last act to be implemented.

And each new thing served to increase the continuing tensions between the Crown and the colonies, coming to a head in 1776.

A few of the most significant events and causes of the revolution are as follows:

- Colonies were opposed to the British trying to exert control over them. Felt that they were infringing on their rights and freedom.
- Didn't like the taxes that Britain imposed on them in order to pay for their defense during the French and Indian War

Taxes were raised steadily through a series of acts over a period of eight years. Stamp Act of 1765, the Townshend Acts of 1767, and the Tea Act of 1773.

The colonists were fiercely opposed to these rising taxes, especially since they had no representation in British Parliament. The colonists were opposed to the British trying to exert more control over them, as they had enjoyed a lot of freedom and rights beforehand. They also resented the British in the motherland, as they tried to make the colonists pay for the French and Indian War when the colonists had been the ones fighting on the front lines.

The Boston Massacre

Tensions continued to rise, and in 1770, the resistance from the colonists spilled into violence. A small group of British soldiers was protecting the customs house. The colonists came to taunt them, but things escalated, with rocks being thrown at the soldiers. A soldier fired, and some of the other soldiers followed, even though no direct order had been given. Five men ultimately died. This event would become known as the Boston Massacre. The poor relationship between the Crown and the colonies was now on display.

As the relationship between Britain and its colonies continued to deteriorate, Americans felt increasingly frustrated. When the Tea Act of 1773 was passed, the Bostonians were fed up enough to find a way to make their frustrations known.

On December 16th, 1773, at Griffin's Wharf, Bostonians seized 342 chests of tea that had just arrived from the British East India

Company and poured it into the Boston Harbor (in today's money, that equates to almost two million dollars). The Boston Tea Party, as it would become known, led to Parliament passing additional laws in the colonies called the Coercive Acts or Intolerable Acts, which were passed in 1774.

Boston Tea Party.
https://commons.wikimedia.org/wiki/File:Destruction_of_tea_at_Boston_Harbor_LCCN9 1795889.jpg

The Boston Tea Party led British Parliament to pass four new acts called the Coercive Acts (they were dubbed the Intolerable Acts in the colonies). They were as follows:

- The Boston Port Act – This act was passed in March 1774 and allowed the British Royal Navy to blockade and cut off commercial traffic from Boston Harbor. Under the act, imports and exports from international ports were forbidden. The only provisions allowed to come through were those used by the British Army and necessities. The blockade would be lifted once Boston paid restitution to the British East India Company for the destroyed tea.

- The Massachusetts Government Act – Under this act, which was passed in May 1774, the Massachusetts government was restructured with people appointed by the British Empire. These people were given more power and authority. It effectively took away the democratic rights of colonists and ensured they had very little say in political matters by not allowing them to vote officials into office. Town meetings also became restricted to just once a year.

- The Administration of Justice Act – This act is also known as the Murder Act and was passed on the same day as the Massachusetts Government Act. The act gave the governor more power to intervene when a British officer was charged with a capital offense. It allowed for the trial to either be moved to another colony or to England so that the offender could have a "fair trial." However, the colonists interpreted this as a way for British officers to get away with crimes, including murder.

- The Quartering Act – This was the final Intolerable Act and was passed in June 1774. Under this act, high-ranking army officers were allowed to demand better quarters for their troops. It also allowed them to refuse accommodations they deemed inconvenient or unacceptable. To add insult to injury, colonists would have to pay for this housing.

The Coercive Acts were implemented to regain control and authority over the unruly colonies. The British sought to punish the rebellious Bostonians and bring the other colonies into line. But the acts did not help. The colonists pushed back and decided to address their concerns head-on with the Crown. They created a delegation to discuss what to do next. In September 1774, the First Continental Congress, made up of George Washington, Patrick Henry, John Jay, John Adams, and Samuel Adams, among many others, met in Philadelphia.

Their demands were simple: they still wanted fair representation (a popular cry was "No taxation without representation") and sought to boycott British goods, hitting the British in their pocketbooks. They wanted the British to ask for their consent, so they sent a letter to British Parliament, asking to rescind the acts.

Before adjourning, the men planned to meet again in May 1775. But by this time, the conflict had turned violent. Only a month before, the Battles of Lexington and Concord had taken place, kicking off the American Revolution.

The biggest causes of strife for the colonists were the lack of representation in the British government and the heavy taxes. The list of grievances was long, but they were angry because their needs and wants were not addressed or represented by the government in Great Britain. They had to pay taxes to a government that did not seem to care about or have any interest in representing them. Britain didn't allow the colonists to trade with other countries. The colonists were completely reliant on the Crown for all their imports. Colonists were also forbidden from expanding beyond the Mississippi River.

With such a long list of complaints, the possibility of armed conflict was high. And eventually, the colonists and British had had enough of the petty bickering and set out to solve the problem through war.

PART TWO: The United States Are Born (1776–1861)

Chapter 5: The American Revolution

As tensions between Great Britain and the colonies in North America continued to escalate, minor skirmishes and conflicts began to take place, eventually setting off the American Revolutionary War.

Battles of Lexington and Concord

The Battles of Lexington and Concord in Massachusetts, where the first shots were fired, would officially mark the beginning of the American Revolution on April 19th, 1775.

Tensions between the colonists and the British Empire had been simmering for many years and were further heightened following the end of the Seven Years' War. Relations reached a breaking point after the British set out a series of acts and British Parliament declared that Massachusetts was openly rebelling against it.

The stage was set for war to break out at any moment. That moment came on April 18th, 1775, when a doctor named Joseph Warren, who was also a member of the Sons of Liberty, found out that Redcoat troops would be marching into Concord that very night. He sent two men, Paul Revere and William Dawes, to let the residents know.

Revere went to Charlestown, a neighborhood in Boston where Patriots were on the lookout for British troops. Two lanterns were hung in the North Church, located in Boston, to signal that the British were coming by sea.

Meanwhile, Dawes went on a separate route to Lexington, which was located a few miles away from Concord. Revere also traveled to Lexington, beating Dawes there since he was closer. The two were joined by Samuel Prescott, a doctor.

They were successful in warning people, but the British authorities were also alerted. Revere was caught. Dawes and Prescott escaped, but only Prescott finished the ride.

The following day, on April 19th, around seven hundred British soldiers arrived in Lexington to find a Patriot arsenal. Seventy-seven militiamen were waiting to stop the British. The militiamen were in the process of retreating when someone fired a shot, leading to additional shots being fired. When the shooting ended, eight militiamen had been killed, and an additional nine were injured. Only one Redcoat was wounded.

The British continued their march into Concord to seize arms and weapons but were surprised to discover the majority of the weapons had already been dispatched elsewhere. Furious, they burned down what they could get their hands on.

Fearing the whole town would be burned, the militiamen advanced on Concord's North Bridge, where a group of British soldiers was defending it. The British fired, and the militiamen fired in return.

Soon, nearly two thousand militiamen had arrived in the area, ready for a battle. They fought hard and with determination, and the British eventually retreated. At Lexington, a fresh group of Redcoats had arrived to support their troops, but the colonists kept their attacks going. Further reinforcements arrived for the militiamen later that evening.

Even though the colonists fought in a disorganized manner and shot out at random, often missing their mark, it was nonetheless a dizzying victory. They had managed to fight back against the powerful British Army. The American Revolution had officially started.

When the Second Continental Congress met again as planned a month later, the delegation had two notable new members: Thomas

Jefferson and Benjamin Franklin.

The First Continental Congress hadn't planned to create a revolution when they decided to meet again in a year, but things had changed. The Second Continental Congress agreed to create a Continental Army, which would be headed by George Washington.

British Allies

Britain tried to form alliances with the slaves in the colonies. Between 1700 and 1775, the population in the colonies had grown from 250,000 people to 2.5 million people. A quarter of this population (one in four people) were slaves. In November 1775, Lord Dunmore, the governor of Virginia, proclaimed that slaves of the rebelling colonists who fought alongside the British would be granted their freedom. The idea of freedom was too good to pass up. Throughout the course of the American Revolution, tens of thousands of Africans fought on the British side. Around five thousand fought on the colonists' side.

Many Native American tribes tried to remain neutral at first, but the majority of the tribes eventually sided with the British, especially when they came under constant attack from the American militia. They were promised great things in return for the services, things that never came to fruition.

Colonial Allies

Surprisingly, the colonists had a lot of allies. The French, the Spanish, and the Dutch eventually helped them fight against the British. Well-known historical figures, such as the Prussian officer Frederick William, the Polish soldier Kazimierz Pulaski, and other notable men helped with the American Revolution.

Perhaps the most well-known personage was Marquis de Lafayette, a French aristocrat who fought with the colonists during the American Revolution. He later played a crucial role in the French Revolution and the July Revolution of 1830.

Born into a noble family, Lafayette became a courtier at King Louis XVI's court, but what he really yearned to be was a soldier. So, he traveled to the colonies on his own at the age of nineteen and became a major general in the Continental Army.

He had no military or battle experience, so Washington took him under his wings, and the two became close friends. Under the guidance of Washington, Lafayette quickly emerged as a man with great skill. He also had great connections to the French court.

Lafayette was eventually given his own division and served the Continental Army well. In 1779, he returned to France and convinced the king to send more supplies, resources, and troops to the colonies to help the Americans, which he did. Lafayette returned to the US in 1780.

Upon Lafayette's return to France in 1782, he was made a brigadier general, and his exemplary performance earned him an honorary citizenship to the US.

George Washington
https://en.wikipedia.org/wiki/George_Washington

The fall and winter of 1775 were tough for Washington's forces, but the capture of Fort Ticonderoga helped to shift the tide in their favor, with British soldiers leaving the city and finding shelter in Canada.

The American Revolution went on for eight years and is peppered with dozens of battles and conflicts, big and small. We don't have the space to look at them all, so we will look at some of the most decisive battles that influenced the war.

The Capture of Fort Ticonderoga – May 10th, 1775

Fort Ticonderoga was located in Lake Champlain in New York, which was an ideal location. It had access to the Hudson River Valley and to Canada, making it a desirable target.

Early in the morning of May 10th, 1775, the British fort was attacked. The surprise offensive was carried out by General Benedict Arnold, who had joined forces with Ethan Allen and the Green Mountain Boys of Vermont.

The attack shook the completely unprepared British soldiers, as it was the first American offensive of the war. Even though it did not escalate into a large-scale conflict, it was a significant victory for the Americans. They captured the fort and took all of the British weapons and artillery.

This was a great moment for General Benedict Arnold and Ethan Allen, both of whom viewed themselves as the hero in the early days of the war. Arnold would go on to betray the Patriots. He defected to the British in 1780 and was planning to give up the US post at West Point to them, but the plot was discovered in time. Allen was captured by the British in 1775 after failing to take Montreal; he was released around three years later.

Benedict Arnold.
https://commons.wikimedia.org/wiki/File:Benedict_Arnold_1color.jpg

Battle of Bunker Hill – June 17th, 1775

Breed's Hill, less than a mile away from Bunker Hill, located in Massachusetts, was the setting of the first real battle of the war. Even though it did not end in a victory for the colonial soldiers, it helped to boost the morale of the Continental Army.

The majority of the colonists had no experience with war and were pitted against experienced British soldiers, yet they managed to hold them off for several hours. The colonists were eventually pushed back by the British, but not before they managed to wound or kill nearly half of the 2,200 soldiers, making it one of the bloodiest battles of the war. Compared to the one thousand Redcoat casualties, only around four hundred Patriots were wounded or killed.

The Battle of Bunker Hill showed the colonists that they could rise to the challenge and do what they needed to do for their country. The British realized the fight wouldn't be as easy as they had initially thought and took less aggressive measures to conserve manpower.

Battle of Fort Washington – November 1776

The Battle of Fort Washington resulted in one of the Patriots' worst defeats during the war. While General George Washington led the Continental Army, Robert Magaw was the man on the battlefield, while General William Howe led the British and Hessian troops. The Americans suffered approximately three thousand casualties (most of whom were captured) and also lost critical supplies and weapons.

Faced with utter defeat, the Continental Army retreated into Delaware, and Howe moved into Fort Washington.

Battles of Trenton and Princeton – December 1776-January 1777

During the American Revolution, Washington won two crucial battles for America within ten days of crossing the Delaware on December 25th, 1776.

One was the Battle of Trenton, which took place on December 26th, 1776. Washington and his troops easily defeated a group of Hessian mercenaries, who were tired and entirely unprepared for Washington's calculated attack. They surrendered quickly with minimal bloodshed. Out of the 1,400 soldiers who made up the Hessian force, only 22 died. Another ninety-two were wounded. On the American side, two soldiers froze to death, and five others were wounded.

Washington realized his men wouldn't be able to hold Trenton against the British Army, so they withdrew into Delaware to bide their time.

On December 30th, Washington crossed the Delaware again and found his army was grossly outnumbered by the British soldiers. Washington managed to raise his number of troops to five thousand and waited at Trenton for the British.

Around 5,500 British soldiers arrived, led by General Charles Cornwallis. The two sides engaged in a series of skirmishes before Cornwallis pulled back for the day, thinking that victory was nearly his.

But Washington wasn't ready to give up. He left behind five hundred troops at the campsite while the rest of the army marched through the night to Princeton, which was located twelve miles away. They walked in the dark without torches and wrapped cloth around the wagon wheels to muffle the noise. Imagine Cornwallis's surprise when he woke up the next morning and discovered their disappearance!

Washington arrived at Princeton, and his troops easily broke through the British defense and won the Battle of Princeton. They continued their march until they arrived at Morristown, where they set up quarters for the winter, away from the British.

These two battles were huge victories for Washington. He had managed to unite soldiers from the different colonies to fight as one, and they had been able to defeat their common enemy as a united force.

Battles of Saratoga – September 19th and October 7th, 1777

Two battles were fought in Saratoga County, New York. During the first battle, the British forces, under General John Burgoyne, emerged victorious. However, the victory cost them dearly. When the British attacked the colonists at Bemis Heights, they were soundly defeated by the Americans and forced to turn back.

This would become the turning point in the revolution. Since 1776, France had been secretly helping the rebel forces fight against the British, with aristocrats like Lafayette supporting their cause. After the victory at Saratoga, France came out from the shadows and publicly pledged its support for the Americans. However, it would be another two years before France formally declared war on Britain.

Soon after these two battles, the British began focusing on the south, as they believed there were more Loyalists there. By late 1778, British troops had taken Savannah, Georgia. In 1780, they took Charleston.

Battle of Yorktown – September 28th–October 19th, 1781

A group of American and French forces cornered the British army in Yorktown. The forces couldn't leave, nor could they receive any additional help because the British fleet had been driven off by the French.

General Charles Cornwallis had no other choice but to surrender. The war was essentially over, even though Charleston and New York City stayed under British control for another few years. Toward the end of 1783, the last of the British soldiers finally left, officially marking the end of the war.

Peace treaties were drafted in Paris in November 1782. The Treaty of Paris was signed on September 3rd, 1783. Britain ceded all control of the colonies and fully recognized them as an independent nation. Under the treaty, Canada remained a British province, which created the northern border of the United States.

However, not all colonists living in America were opposed to the British; they were called Loyalists. The Loyalists mostly stayed out of the war, but once the war officially ended, approximately 100,000 Loyalists left America and either went to Britain or settled in other British colonies, such as Canada.

Post-Revolution Territorial Changes

Founding Fathers

The Revolutionary War ended as a success story for the United States due to the collective efforts of all the colonies and outside nations. However, there were a number of men, known as the Founding Fathers, who are historically seen as having played a key role in securing the country's independence.

There were many men who could be considered Founding Fathers, but seven stand out the most. This is, by no means, a comprehensive list of the Founding Fathers, but it gives you a good idea of what kind of men the nation looked up to.

- George Washington: He led the Continental Army and became the first president of the United States.
- Thomas Jefferson: He was a diplomat to France, where he earned its help in the war. He drafted the Declaration of Independence and was the first secretary of the state, the second vice president, and the third president.
- John Adams: He became the second president of the US and served as vice president twice. He was a prolific writer and lawyer.
- Benjamin Franklin: He was a notable inventor, writer, printer, and intellectual. He served as a diplomat to France and Sweden and was the first postmaster general.
- Alexander Hamilton: Best remembered for his infamous duel with Aaron Burr, Hamilton was the first secretary of the treasury. He promoted the idea of a central bank and was a prolific writer, crafting almost all of *The Federalist Papers*, which were essays to garner support for the US Constitution.
- John Jay: He was the first chief justice. He helped create the Constitution and wrote some articles for *The Federalist Papers*. He helped craft foreign policy after the war.
- James Madison: He became the fourth president of the US. He was a major contributor to the Constitution and Bill of Rights.

The Founding Fathers.
https://en.wikipedia.org/wiki/File:Declaration_of_Independence_(1819),_by_John_Trumbull.jpg

Their writings on life and liberty, as well as their actions and thoughts, provided the foundation upon which the newly independent country was built. What is remarkable is that most of these men were all young men in their thirties and forties by the end of the war. There were a few outliers, like Washington, who was in his early fifties, and Franklin, who was in his seventies.

Their contributions were not simply idealistic. Washington led an army during the revolution, and Thomas Jefferson wrote the Declaration of Independence. John Jay was a chief justice in the Supreme Court, and Hamilton was secretary of the treasury. They didn't just put words on paper; they followed through and tried to achieve what they thought would benefit the country the most.

The Founding Fathers had an idea of what a free, independent country should be like, and they used those ideas to create the American nation. They managed to do what many European colonies dreamed of: independence from the motherland.

Unfortunately, their ideals were not always fair and placed greater emphasis on ensuring the rights and liberties of white landowning men rather than all Americans. Many of them owned slaves and placed a lesser value on their lives. They also weren't always united in their beliefs, which led to friction.

However, the legacy they left behind cannot be denied. Subsequent generations used their foundation for equality to fight for minorities and the disadvantaged. Today, for the most part, Americans enjoy the same liberties, protections, and freedoms.

Chapter 6: The Constitution and the Bill of Rights

The Constitution, written in 1787 and ratified in 1788, is perhaps the most important law in the United States. It is also the world's oldest national constitution still in use today.

James Madison is the Founding Father credited with drafting the Constitution and the Bill of Rights. However, even Madison admitted that many other people contributed to the creation of the documents.

When the Constitution was drafted, the main purpose was to give the government enough power to run the country. However, the government had limits so that it could not infringe upon the people's fundamental rights.

The federal government was separated into three different branches: legislative, executive, and judicial. Checks were put in place to ensure that the power of all three branches would stay balanced. The powers of each branch are vested by the Congress (legislative branch), the president (executive branch), and the Supreme Court and federal courts (judicial branch). A clause was also put into the Constitution so it could be amended should the need arise.

Roman Influences

Ancient Rome was one of the biggest sources of inspiration for the Founding Fathers when they were deciding on the best form of government. Rome was initially ruled by a king, but once the monarchy was abolished, the country became a republic.

The Roman Republic was a sort of golden era, especially in terms of democratic principles, as it saw Rome rise in prominence. As many of you know, Rome became a power to be reckoned with. This period of history was studied extensively in the Western world. Most educated Americans' studies included ancient Roman literature and the philosophies around liberty, power, and freedom.

Therefore, it is not surprising that the Founding Fathers had similar views on what an ideal American government would look like. Similarities were often drawn between Rome and America since both fought to become free from tyrannical rulers. As such, the political system for the new world was influenced greatly by the Roman Republic.

Constitution

The US Constitution was drafted and finalized on September 17th, 1787. It was signed by thirty-nine of the fifty-five delegates. Some refused to sign it because the Constitution did not include a Bill of Rights (this would be added later). One delegate refused to sign the document because the Constitution protected the slave trade.

The first real form of government was the Second Continental Congress. On July 4th, 1776, after a formal declaration of their independence from the Crown, it acted as an interim government. The Second Continental Congress drafted the Articles of Confederation, which outlined the functions and responsibilities of the government. This was the document that preceded the Constitution.

Once the United States was formed, George Washington soon realized that something stronger than the Articles of Confederation was needed. With his encouragement, the process of drafting a constitution was started. The new document replaced the original Articles of Confederation. The biggest difference between the two documents was the three separate branches of government.

The US Constitution.
https://en.wikipedia.org/wiki/File:Constitution_of_the_United_States,_page_1.jpg

Bill of Rights

Although the Constitution was eventually adopted, it was not a painless process. Support for the Constitution was divided between the Federalists and the anti-Federalists.

The Federalists were in support of the Constitution and pushed to have it ratified. They believed in the need for a strong union and a centralized government. The group was made up of wealthy bankers, businessmen, and other professionals.

Anti-Federalists, on the other hand, did not see a need to create a new document as they thought the Articles of Confederation was enough. They did not want a stronger central government, as they feared an overly powerful government would pose a threat to people's individual rights and liberties. This group was made up of laborers, small farmers, shopkeepers, and others who were understandably worried about not having a voice.

The pushback from the anti-Federalists eventually led to the implementation of the first ten amendments. The amendments were introduced by James Madison, and although twelve were produced, only ten were ratified. These amendments make up the Bill of Rights, and they guarantee the following rights to all American citizens:[1]

- Freedom to practice one's religion, the freedom of speech, and the freedom of the press;
- The right to bear arms;
- No quartering of soldiers;
- Freedom from unreasonable searches and seizures;
- Right to due process;
- Rights to a speedy trial if accused of a crime;
- Right to be tried by a jury;
- Freedom from any cruel or unusual punishments;
- Other rights of the people;
- Powers reserved to the states.

In short, the Bill of Rights ensures individual freedoms and liberties cannot be infringed upon by the government on a whim.

Levels of Government

Under the Constitution, the federal government was separated into three distinct branches to ensure an equal division of power and authority.

---

[1] "Bill of Rights: The Really Short Version."
https://users.csc.calpoly.edu/~jdalbey/Public/Bill_of_Rights.html.

The branches are as follows:

- **Legislative (Congress)**

This branch is made up of the House of Representatives, the Senate, and special agencies that help with work passed in Congress. These agencies include the Copyright Office, Government Accountability Office, and US Capitol Police, to name a few.

Congress drafts new laws and has the power to declare war. It is also responsible for confirming or rejecting nominees for federal agencies and the Supreme Court. Members of Congress hold debates and investigations to make sure the country's governing apparatus works efficiently and is free of corruption. Members of Congress are voted in by the public.

- **Executive**

The responsibility for carrying out and enforcing the laws lies with the executive branch. This branch is made up of three key roles, with the most famous role being that of the president.

The president is voted into office by the public, although, technically, the electoral college votes the president in. The public votes, and the party with the most votes wins that state's batch of votes for the electoral college. Different states have different numbers of electoral votes based on the number of people that state has in Congress.

It is the president's job to lead the country and government. They are supported by the vice president and the Cabinet. In the event that the president can't serve, the vice president steps into the role. Today, presidents can only serve a maximum of two terms; however, vice presidents do not have that cap. They can serve for any number of terms.

The Cabinet includes the vice president and other high-ranking public servants and heads of executive departments. Each member of the Cabinet is appointed by the president, although the Senate must approve the nomination with a vote.

The bulk of the work in this branch is carried out by government departments and public servants.

- Judicial

The third branch of the US government is responsible for interpreting and applying the country's federal laws and legislations. The courts also decide if any laws are in violation of the Constitution.

Federal courts and the Supreme Court fall under the judicial branch. According to the Constitution, Congress is the authoritative power that can establish federal courts.

Judges in the Supreme Court are appointed through a nomination from the president. The nomination must be debated and then voted on by the Senate.

As you can see, the three branches of government, while quite distinct and separate, are intertwined and work closely together. The Founding Fathers believed that dividing up power in such a way would ensure that the government would always act in the best interest of the people and society.

The First President of the United States

Once the country was created, the electoral college was faced with a daunting prospect: who was going to lead the country? Today, presidents are voted into office every four years through an election, but no such process was in place back in 1788.

The first election was an extremely simple and straightforward affair, quite unlike the current presidential elections. A few months after the Constitution was ratified on June 21st, 1788, the electoral college took a vote, and a unanimous decision was made to elect George Washington as president.

Washington was not keen to become president. In fact, after the Revolutionary War ended and the Treaty of Paris was signed, his plan was to retire from public life. But the pressures and demands of the public outweighed his own desires, and he took on the mantle. His work as the head of the Constitution committee was especially impressive, as was the way he had conducted himself in battles during the revolution. The delegates were convinced they had their first president.

John Adams, another candidate for the role of president, was elected as the first vice president. (For a time, the vice presidency was awarded to the man who had the second highest number of votes; this changed under Jefferson.) Washington and Adams formally came into office on April 30th, 1789. Because Washington, DC, did not yet exist, the inauguration took place in New York City.

George Washington's inauguration.
https://commons.wikimedia.org/wiki/File:Washington%27s_Inauguration.jpg

It was a great honor and an immense burden all at once. How was he going to lead a brand-new country that was fresh out of a war with Britain? By cutting ties with Great Britain, the United States had embarked on a journey to embrace democracy, which was a rare notion in a world filled with kings, empires, and royals seeking more and more power. Democracy was great in theory, but Washington had to figure out how to show that a country could run on those ideals.

After Washington's first term in office ended, he was elected unanimously once again on February 13th, 1793, to lead the country once more. During his time in office, he helped shape the executive branch and define the roles and responsibilities for the roles in that branch. He knew he would be setting a precedent for how future presidents would conduct themselves, and he was determined to set a stellar example as a fair and honest man with strong principles and integrity. Wishing to keep the US out of any global conflicts, he typically maintained a neutral stance in foreign affairs, even when the French Revolution broke out.

Some men, like Thomas Jefferson, believed the US should help its former ally, especially considering that the French were trying to install their own version of democracy. But Washington believed neutrality was the best option considering the French didn't seem to have a firm plan in place with how to proceed once the revolution was over.

Washington's presidency was marked with several firsts. He was the one who signed a bill to establish a permanent capital city in the US. It was named Washington, DC, after him. He established the first national bank, set up the presidential Cabinet, nominated the first judge for the country's Supreme Court, and signed a law protecting authors' copyrights.

What Americans know as Thanksgiving Day is the national holiday Washington created to celebrate both the end of the Revolutionary War and the ratification of the Constitution. It is held on the fourth Thursday of November every year.

Under his presidency, the Bill of Rights was ratified, and the United States expanded to include five more states: Vermont, Kentucky, North Carolina, Rhode Island, and Tennessee. To this day, Washington remains one of the most influential people in American history. He set an example that was hard to follow for some, and he consistently ranks as one of the best presidents.

Chapter 7: The Louisiana Purchase and the War of 1812

Louisiana

The Louisiana territory was first discovered by Spanish explorer Hernando de Soto in 1541 while he was exploring the Mississippi River. But it was claimed in 1682 by a French explorer named René-Robert Cavelier, although Native Americans had been living in the area by that point for thousands of years. The region was named after Louis XIV.

In 1762, Louisiana went to Spain as part of the negotiations to end the Seven Years' War. Under the terms of the Treaty of Fontainebleau, Louisiana was given to Spain. But in 1800, Napoleon forced the country to give up the territory, which it did under the Treaty of San Ildefonso.

The plan was to build a French force and have it stationed in Louisiana to defend "New France" against British or American attacks. France wanted to expand its empire in North America.

While this was happening, slaves in Haiti began to revolt against the French. While dealing with this revolution, Napoleon was also fighting the Napoleonic Wars in Europe. He desperately needed money for the war, so he made the decision to sell Louisiana, bringing a permanent end to France's desire to expand its North American empire.

The territory was purchased from the French First Republic by the United States for $15 million (around $309 million in present-day dollars). The transaction was negotiated by a treaty confirming the purchase was signed in Paris, France, in 1803.

The land was located to the west of the Mississippi River and was enormous, measuring approximately 828,000 square miles. It included the Rocky Mountains, went up the Gulf of Mexico, and stretched all the way to the Canadian border. It was so big that it doubled the size of the existing country. As you might already know (or have guessed), present-day Louisiana is much smaller than the original territory.

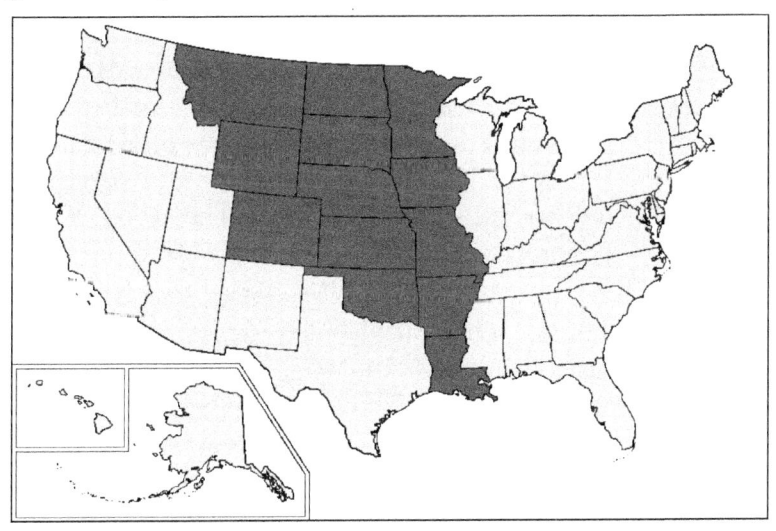

States that likely would have been included in the Louisiana Purchase.

MaGioZal, based on an image by Wikimedia Commons user Brianski, which is itself based on an image by Wikimedia Commons user Roke and Wikimedia Commons user Brianski., CC BY-SA 3.0 <http://creativecommons.org/licenses/by-sa/3.0/>, via Wikimedia Commons; https://commons.wikimedia.org/wiki/File:United_States_Louisiana_Purchase_states.png

What did the purchase of the territory mean for the US? Well, the French only owned a small piece of the territory, as most of it was inhabited by Native Americans. The US government had the right to get the land from the indigenous people either through force or cooperation.

The purchase was a smart decision. The land was rich in natural resources and strategically placed next to an important waterway, the Mississippi River. New Orleans was an important port city that had a rich culture, being influenced by French, Spanish, and African cultures. Now, the US had control of the city, and the country looked to continue its expansion.

The War of 1812

Causes

While the United States tried to stay out of global conflicts to instead focus on expanding and cementing its own nation, petty conflicts continued to rage in Europe. Things were especially tense between Great Britain and France. Despite America's best attempts to stay out of the Napoleonic Wars, they were dragged into the escalating conflict for a number of reasons.

Chief among them was that both France and Great Britain tried to stop the US from trading with each other. Great Britain even went as far as to pass an order in 1807 requiring neutral countries to have a license before they could trade with France or any of its colonies. This did not sit well with the US. The Royal Navy also began to practice impressment, where sailors were removed from US ships and forced to work on British vessels.

President Thomas Jefferson decided to counter Britain by placing restrictions on imports. In 1807, he passed the Embargo Act, which closed all of America's ports to exports. Jefferson's hope was to teach France and especially Britain a lesson by showing them how much they depended on American goods. He wanted them to accept his country's neutral stance, and he wanted Britain to stop the impressment of sailors.

The Embargo Act was a complete failure and only served to hurt America's economy, which saw exports fall from $108 million to $22 million in under a year. Congress decided to repeal the act and replaced it with the Non-Intercourse Act. Under this act, America could trade with any country except France and Britain. This came with its own set of problems.

Finally, a bill was introduced in May 1810 that changed things. The US pledged that if one country removed its restrictions against America, then the US would, in turn, place restrictions against the other country. When France dropped its restrictions against the US, the US resumed its restrictions against Great Britain.

War Begins

While the US was dealing with a potential conflict with Britain, it was also facing issues at home with the Native Americans. The Americans were looking to expand their territory but were met with resistance and hostility from the natives.

In 1809, the Treaty of Fort Wayne was agreed upon. Under the treaty, several Native American tribes had to sell three million acres of land in what is now Ohio, Michigan, Indiana, and Illinois to the US; in return, the Native Americans would receive two cents per acre.

Although the Native Americans involved in the process agreed to the treaty (at least for the most part), not all of the tribes in those lands were consulted, namely the Shawnee. Tecumseh, a Shawnee leader, spoke against the treaty and warned the Americans to stop encroaching on their land. He eventually organized a group of Native Americans to fight back against the relentless expansion of white settlers.

Governor William Henry Harrison (a future US president) organized one thousand troops to march into Prophetstown. This village was named after Tecumseh's brother, who called himself the "Prophet." He believed he was meant to lead the natives to rise up against the settlers, who had introduced evil vices and turned the natives away from their culture.

The fighting that ensued from November 7th, 1811, became known as the Battle of Tippecanoe. Tecumseh was away during the battle, and when he returned home, he found the village in ruins. Angry and defeated, Tecumseh decided to side with the British in the hopes they would stop the Americans from further expanding on their lands.

In the meantime, Congress was being pressured by the War Hawks to make a decision about a war with Britain. The War Hawks were a group of young politicians who were itching for a confrontation with Great Britain. They were hoping that by fighting the British, they could increase territorial gains in Canada and any other British-protected lands.

To their joy, the president, James Madison, finally declared war on Britain on June 18th, 1812. However, not everyone was happy about this decision. But happy or not, in the long run, the war would be a crucial point in America's history and demonstrate its growth as a country.

The Siege of Detroit – August 1812

As a colony of Great Britain, Canada became the first target of the American forces. American troops, led by William Hull, prepared to invade. Their goal was to capture Montreal. However, Hull felt it would be best to use Fort Detroit as their base and attack from there. He expected a swift victory.

However, he soon began to get nervous, especially since he was faced with the indigenous population who would not hesitate to take up arms against the US troops.

The battle was led by Sir Isaac Brock, a British soldier. He was supported by Native American allies led by Tecumseh. Sensing Hull's hesitation, he pressed forward and used Hull's fears about the natives to his advantage.

Brock and Tecumseh played mind games by making him believe they had a bigger army than they actually did and making him feel as if he was surrounded. Hull fell for the bluff and surrendered Detroit, Michigan, as well as his troop. The number of deaths was minimal, and Hull did not put up a big resistance.

The battle ended in a humiliating defeat for the Americans and wasn't a great start to the war, especially considering Fort Mackinac in what is now Michigan had already fallen with a single shot being fired.

The loss of Detroit brought all plans to invade Canada to a standstill. It was a critical point for the Americans because their war strategy had just fallen apart.

The Battle of Lake Erie – September 1813

Although American troops did not fare well in land battles, they excelled in naval fights. The Battle of Lake Erie is a great example of the Americans' might on water. The US Navy, under the guidance of Captain Oliver Hazard Perry, took on the British Royal Navy near Put-in-Bay, Ohio.

The Royal Navy was the largest navy in the world, so it might be surprising to hear that the US Navy was able to defeat them on multiple occasions. However, Britain was fighting against Napoleon in Europe, so most of its resources were concentrated there.

In the Battle of Lake Erie, the US was able to successfully prevent the British from taking control of Lake Erie. It was an important victory for the Americans, both morally and strategically, because they ensured the lake remained theirs.

Bolstered by this victory, they turned their attention to Detroit, which was recaptured after the Battle of the Thames. Tecumseh died in that battle, breaking the Native American confederacy. Although the natives continued to help the British on a small scale, they were no longer united.

The End of the War

Since the start of the war, the US Navy had won a number of victories against the British navy, but by April 1814, Napoleon had been defeated. Great Britain now had the luxury to pour all its efforts into the war against America.

Over the spring and summer, a large number of British troops poured into North America and made their way to Washington, DC. On August 24th, 1814, the British marched into the capital, setting fire to key monuments and buildings, such as the White House and the Capitol building. A few days later, a massive storm swept through (some think it might have been a hurricane), extinguishing the flames and wrecking British ships.

The Treaty of Ghent

Less than a month later, on September 11th, the American navy defeated the British fleet on Lake Champlain. Two days later, Fort McHenry in Baltimore held steady as the Royal Navy bombed them for over twenty-four hours. Discouraged by their lack of progress, the British left Chesapeake Bay and turned their attention toward New Orleans. Francis Scott Key was so moved by the sight of bombs bursting in the air that he wrote the "Star-Spangled Banner."

In the meantime, British officials had already begun talks to negotiate for peace. The negotiations were finalized in the Treaty of Ghent, which was signed in late December 1814. Under the terms, any territory conquered during the war had to be returned to its rightful owner. The boundaries of Canada and the US would also be formally determined. Impressment and the rights of neutral US ships and vessels were not discussed in the treaty. However, the treaty allowed the US to continue expanding in the Great Lakes region.

Because news of the treaty did not reach North America immediately, British forces in America continued their campaign. On January 8th, 1815, a major battle took place in New Orleans. British troops suffered another defeat. The US troops were led by Andrew Jackson, who would eventually become the president of the United States.

Although the treaty had not provided any resolutions to the main causes of the war, the Americans still considered it to be a victory, even though the war was technically a stalemate. However, it is hard to discount what the Americans achieved. They had taken on the greatest navy in the world and came out as the clear winners.

Effects of the War of 1812

In America's long and colorful history, the War of 1812 was certainly not a hugely impactful war. However, it helped shape the country in the years to come.

The Treaty of Ghent helped put an end to partisan infighting and led to the demise of the Federalist Party. Many felt their reluctance to enter the war had been unpatriotic. Winning the war was a huge boost to American nationalism and their sense of not needing anyone else to survive and thrive. It also further solidified their intent to expand and grow, which would become their primary focus in the 19th century.

Chapter 8: Expansion in the West and South

Monroe Doctrine

As the United States continued to expand and began to firmly establish itself globally as an independent nation, it wanted to make sure its future would stay secure. So, President James Monroe issued the Monroe Doctrine in 1823.

President Monroe.
https://commons.wikimedia.org/wiki/File:James_Monroe_White_House_portrait_1819.jpg

The doctrine would form a key part of American foreign policy. It basically made it clear that no outside powers were allowed to meddle in the Americas.

Four key points made up the doctrine. They are as follows:

- The United States would stay out of Europe's affairs.
- The United States would not interfere with any existing colony in the Americas.
- No further attempts at European colonization in the Western Hemisphere would be allowed.
- The US government would view any European power trying to meddle in the Americas as a hostile act.

In short, the US wanted to be left alone, and in exchange, it pledged to do the same. It would be the beginning of America's isolationism policy and its reluctance to get involved in external affairs. It was a policy that would have a significant effect on both world wars.

Over the years, additional changes were made to the Monroe Doctrine. Although the Monroe Doctrine is technically not used today, its principles can still be seen in American foreign policies.

Florida

Much has been discussed in the previous chapters about the British and French colonies, but what about the Spanish colonies?

One of the earliest explorers of what would become the United States, Juan Ponce de León, a Spaniard, discovered the modern-day state of Florida in 1513. Because the land was so vibrant and beautiful, he called it Pascua Florida in honor of Easter (the name means "Flowery Easter"). Early European settlers came to Florida, making it one of the first American frontiers.

Florida would have one of the most colorful histories of the US state, as it changed hands numerous times. For three centuries (from the 16th to the 19th century), Florida was under Spanish rule except for a brief period in the 18th century when it was ruled by Britain due to Spain siding with France during the French and Indian War. Once the American Revolution was over and the Treaty of Paris was signed, Florida was returned to Spain. But things were far from peaceful, and boundary issues continued to plague

Spain.

After several years of negotiating, Spain and the US signed the Adams-Onís Treaty. Spain agreed to cede East Florida to the US and gave up any claims to West Florida. In exchange, the US agreed to pay out claims of damages to US citizens on behalf of Spain. The total cost was roughly $5 million.

Florida was initially a Spanish colony. During the Seven Years' War, Spain gave Florida to Britain. The British divided Florida into East and West. They held onto Florida until 1783, when Britain ceded Florida to Spain.

Disagreements over who owned Florida continued for some, but ultimately, the US gained the territory. In 1822, Florida officially became a US territory and then became the twenty-seventh state in 1845.

The Seminole Wars

The Seminole Wars played a significant role in the cession of Florida. It was also not one of the proudest moments in American history since the series of wars basically served to eject an entire group of people from the land.

In 1817, American authorities were on a mission to recapture slaves who had run away from their owners and were living among a group of Native Americans called the Seminoles. The charge was led by General Andrew Jackson, and American troops forced themselves into the lands occupied by the Seminoles. They burned villages and towns and seized Pensacola and St. Marks, two cities held by Spain.

During this first of the three Seminole Wars, the US convinced Spain the best thing for it would be to cede its territory in Florida, which it did under the Adams-Onís Treaty.

In 1835, the Second Seminole War broke out when the majority of the Seminole population refused to relocate to another area near the Mississippi River. They did not want to leave their reservation near Lake Okeechobee, a space that had been specifically established for them. But wanting to expand their territory, the Americans needed the Seminoles to leave. The Indian Removal Act was established to get rid of them and other Native American tribes living in the Southeast.

Seminole warriors, led by their chief, Osceola, valiantly defended their home. The war finally ended when Osceola was captured by the Americans while parleying with them. The Seminoles stopped resisting after that, and most of them eventually agreed to leave the area.

The Third Seminole War lasted for three years (1855-1858), but the American government was determined to get rid of every last Seminole in Florida. There was very little violence or resistance. Most left on their own, and some were paid to leave. A couple of hundred Seminoles remained in the swamps of Florida. However, their numbers were small, and they remained hidden where the settlers couldn't find them. Florida was finally ready for US expansion.

The Trail of Tears (1830-1850)

The Seminole Wars bring to light another important event: the forceful removal of Native Americans from their homes. Native Americans had been living on the land that would eventually become part of the United States for generations. But by the end of the 1830s, most natives had been pushed westward.

The US government wanted the valuable land the natives were living on. The American settlers could grow cotton and other crops in the rich and fertile land. Gold was discovered in some Native American territories, creating a mad rush to stake claims. The settlers were increasingly encroaching on native territories, leading to skirmishes between both sides. It seemed as if the tensions would never be solved. Newspapers and stories painted Native Americans as either noble savages or a menace to civilization. Americans were both scared and resentful of the natives and wanted a solution to the "Indian problem."

One suggestion, which was even made by George Washington, was to Westernize the Native Americans and make them more like white settlers. This way, they could assimilate better. This method was adopted in some southeastern states.

But in other parts of the country, the Americans forced the Native Americans to leave their homes through violence. They destroyed their villages, looted their homes, and committed mass murder. This is not to say the Native Americans weren't guilty of atrocities as well; sometimes, the US troops took violent measures to act against the violence the Native Americans had committed. Regardless, some Native Americans were forcibly and violently pushed out of their homelands.

Andrew Jackson had long been a great advocate of removing Native Americans. When he became president of the US, he signed the Indian Removal Act of 1830. The act officially gave the government the authority to take away the valuable land held by the Native Americans in the Southeast in exchange for a designated Indian Territory in the West. The Native Americans that were targeted were called the "Five Civilized Tribes." They had been greatly Westernized, showing that even the idea of Westernizing tribes would not work in the United States.

Under the act, the government had to negotiate removal and do so in a peaceful manner. However, more often than not, Native Americans were coerced to move west under the threat of violence. The Choctaw were the first to leave. They left during the winter of 1831. Some were placed in chains, and many had no food, water, or basic supplies. The trip was long, and many died. Perhaps none suffered more than the Cherokee. It is thought that nearly four thousand Cherokee died on the Trail of Tears.

Their problems didn't end when they reached their destination of Oklahoma either. The Indian Territory was already inhabited by other tribes. The Native Americans also had to figure out how to eke a living in this new territory. Although the US government and charities gave assistance, their efforts often were not enough. This is especially prevalent with the boarding schools that were established, which stripped native children of their traditional culture (language, clothing, religion, etc.) to make them more European. This led to the erasure of their culture and their ostracization from their native community. They also weren't fully accepted by the white settlers either, making them straddle two worlds they didn't fit into. Native Americans would not become US citizens until 1924.

Second Great Awakening

While the government was focused on expanding the country and dealing with political reforms and changes, a great social reform was also being undertaken. In the late 18th century, a wave of Protestant religious revival swept across the United States. This wave is called the Second Great Awakening. Religious meetings and church became an integral part of people's lives.

The idea of needing to save one's soul took hold of people and led to numerous moral and social reforms. Some of these reforms included temperance, the emancipation of women, and the abolition of slavery. The reforms not only helped shape society and the lives of Americans, but they also had a deep impact on political and government policies. This would be seen clearly with the issue of the annexation of Texas.

Texas Revolution

Like Florida, Texas was initially explored by a Spaniard. Alonso Álvarez de Piñeda was the first to explore what would become Texas.

For the most part, Texas was largely ignored by European settlers until Spain became nervous that France might want to take it over. So, the Spanish tried to set up a few missions. Their attempt was a failure due to resistance from the Native Americans.

The Spaniards went back to Mexico and didn't think of Texas again until French settlers began to arrive in Louisiana. By 1718, San Antonio had been established by Spain, but tensions with the natives continued.

Believing that a bigger population would help their cause, Spain allowed large numbers of Americans and Europeans to immigrate to Texas in 1820. This led to a rapid increase in the population, but it also started to make Mexico, which gained independence shortly after the first immigrants arrived in Texas, worried because many of the new settlers had no respect for Mexican law. The American government also actively tried to purchase Texas. By 1832, many people in Texas began to openly disobey Mexican laws and revolt against the country. Mexico was also dealing with problems of its own, as its government was unstable.

Rising tensions eventually led to the Texas Revolution. For several months, the Texans fought violently against Mexican troops.

The Battle of the Alamo

The Battle of the Alamo was a significant conflict during the Texan Revolution. The battle started on February 23rd, 1836, and ended on March 6th.

In December 1835, a group of volunteer soldiers in Texas decided to occupy the Alamo, a former mission. The mission had been built by Spanish settlers in the early 18th century. It was used to house missionaries and converts for around seven decades before all of the Spanish missions became secularized in 1793.

Soon after, Spanish troops began to make use of the chapel in the former mission as a fort. In 1821, Mexico gained its independence. Soldiers from the Alamo Company (with Alamo meaning "cottonwood" in Spanish) called the fort the "Alamo" after their hometown of Alamo de Parras.

The Battle of the Alamo is probably the most well-known event of the Texas Revolution. When the Texan soldiers made the decision to occupy the fort in late 1835, they knew this would anger the Mexicans. And on February 23rd, an army of Mexican soldiers led by General Antonio López de Santa Anna (who would become president of Mexico several times and played a pivotal role in the Mexican-American War) marched to the Alamo to seize it.

For nearly two weeks, the Texans managed to hold them at bay, but on March 6th, the Mexican forces were able to breach the fort and take down the Texans. Almost everyone was killed; there were only fourteen survivors.

But instead of breaking the Texans' spirit, what happened at the Alamo only solidified their desire to become independent. The battle became a symbol of resistance and courage. On April 21st, when Sam Houston and his men defeated and captured many of Santa Anna's forces in the Battle of San Jacinto, they cried, "Remember the Alamo" while attacking.

The win at San Jacinto cinched the independence of Texas. Santa Anna was taken prisoner. A declaration of independence was quickly signed after defeating Mexico, making Texas a republic on March 2nd, 1836. However, Mexico refused to recognize the independence of Texas and instead viewed it as a rebellious province. The majority of the Texas population wanted to become a part of the United States, and within a year of becoming a republic, Texas was trying to get annexed by the country.

However, friction between opposition parties and differing views on the practice of slavery delayed the process. Abolition was already a hotly debated issue within Congress, and the Democrats and the

Whigs were fiercely opposed to adding Texas, a pro-slavery state, to the Union since it would upset the balance of free and slave states. They also did not want to anger Mexico, where slavery had been abolished. The Mexicans also continued to refuse to recognize Texas as an independent state.

By this time, the days of electing a president through a simple vote were long gone, and political parties had emerged. In the late 1820s, the Democratic Party emerged. Members of this party were initially part of the Democratic-Republican Party, which was founded in 1792. Over time, the party began to crumble and was eventually split into two parties: the Democrats and the Whigs. The two parties had their differences of opinion, but they were united behind one cause: Texas should not be a part of the United States.

Annexation of Texas

For almost a decade, the annexation of Texas continued to be a political issue, and the great debate dragged on. The eighth president of the US, Martin Van Buren, saw Texas as a huge liability and rejected the annexation proposal. The matter was laid to rest for some time.

However, annexation came up again when William Henry Harrison was elected president in 1840. He only served for thirty-two days before dying, making his vice president, John Tyler, the president.

President Tyler once again opened up the conversation around annexation as part of his expansionist agenda. Texas became his primary focus because he was convinced it would win him a second term. There were also fears that Texas might threaten American security if it was left to its own devices.

In the meantime, the economic situation in Texas was steadily becoming critical. In the early 1840s, Sam Houston, the president of Texas, decided to try and reconcile with Mexico using Britain as a mediator. He wanted Mexico to officially recognize Texas as a republic or allow them to function independently within the Mexican borders. In exchange, Texas would emancipate its slaves.

As they opened these discussions, talks were also secretly being held with the US to become part of the Union, where the political climate had shifted somewhat. When Mexico got wind of this, it told Congress if the US went ahead with the annexation, all diplomatic ties between the two countries would be broken, and war would be declared.

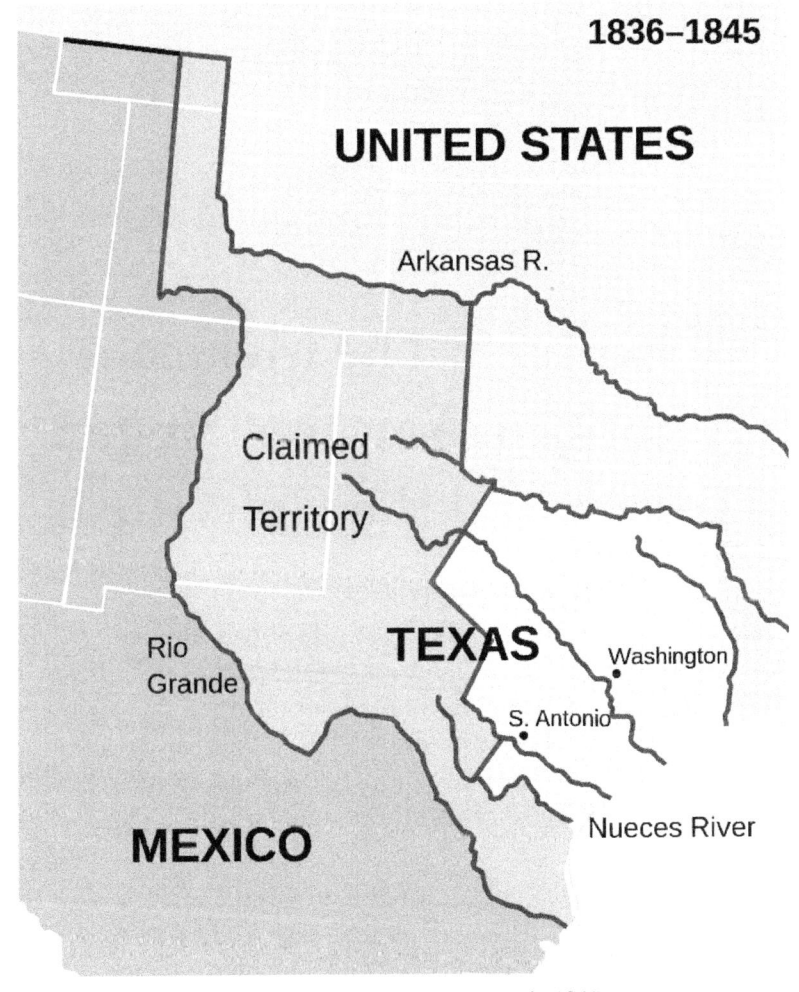

Texas boundaries after annexation in 1845.
This file is licensed under the Creative Commons Attribution-Share Alike 3.0 Unported license; https://en.wikipedia.org/wiki/File:Wpdms_republic_of_texas.svg

Texas remained a republic for almost ten years, but its annexation finally happened on December 29th, 1845, the same year James K Polk became the eleventh president of the United States.

Chapter 9: The Mexican-American War, the Oregon Treaty, and the Gold Rush

Causes of the Mexican-American War

As many in the US had predicted and foreseen, the annexation of Texas angered Mexico and led to a breakdown in the relationship between the two countries. In addition to the annexation of Texas, the two countries were also embroiled in a dispute about the borders of Texas. According to the US, the Rio Grande formed the southern border of Texas. But Mexico contended the Nueces River was the boundary.

California also became a hot issue, as President Polk wanted to continue America's expansion all the way to the Pacific Ocean, believing it to be the country's destiny. Manifest Destiny was the idea that the US was destined by God to settle North America.

And on top of all of this, Mexico had defaulted on its payments to the US. It had promised to pay nearly $3 million to Americans whose properties had been damaged or destroyed as a result of the Texas Revolution.

A combination of these issues eventually led to an all-out war. But before the war began, Polk had offered to purchase California and New Mexico. When Mexico refused the offer, American troops moved into the hotly debated area between the Nueces River and the Rio Grande. In the past, everyone had recognized this as rightfully being a part of Coahuila, a Mexican state.

A series of small-scale skirmishes began on April 25th, 1846. American and Mexican forces fought the Battle of Palo Alto and the Battle of Resaca de la Palma.

The Mexicans were easily defeated in both battles, but Polk made it clear to Congress that they had to do more. On May 13th, Congress approved of declaring war. Some lawmakers were against this declaration, but it was too late, as the US and Mexico were officially at war.

The Mexican-American War

The number of Mexican people living north of the Rio Grande was relatively small. The population was estimated at approximately seventy-five thousand. The US troops advancing into the area were able to conquer the territory easily with little to no resistance. The city of Monterrey was captured just as easily.

Around this time, General Antonio López de Santa Anna came back into the picture. He had been a charismatic and popular leader who headed the government in Mexico eleven times and styled himself as the "Napoleon of the West." In 1835, he repealed the Mexican Constitution, which essentially led to the start of the Texas Revolution. After the revolution ended, he was held captive in Texas for around three weeks. He was forced to sign a humiliating treaty that gave up Texas. He was eventually allowed to return to Mexico.

Santa Anna was soon given control of the army again. He would become president off and on from 1839 to 1844. He ruled like a dictator. In 1844, Santa Anna, who was scared for his life, stepped down from power because of rising tensions over how he ruled. He was captured by a group of Native Americans, who handed him over to the authorities, who then forced him into exile.

He was in exile in Cuba when the war between Mexico and America started. Santa Anna promised Polk that if he came back to Mexico, he would make sure the US came out as the winner in the peace agreements. Mexico had also set aside its anger toward Santa Anna and wanted him to return to lead the charge.

When Santa Anna returned, he took control of the Mexican Army and led it against the US. He had no intentions of honoring his promise to Polk. During the Battle of Buena Vista in February 1847, the American troops crushed Mexico, forcing them to retreat.

There were several significant battles, but every one ended the same. The Mexican troops put up a valiant fight but suffered too many casualties. They suffered from poor leadership and were no match for the American troops.

A year into the war, it was becoming clear that the war was over. It was equally clear who the winners were.

Treaty of Guadalupe Hidalgo

In September 1847, the Mexican government formally surrendered after the fall of Mexico City, and negotiations for peace began. The Treaty of Guadalupe Hidalgo was finalized and signed on February 2nd, 1848. The terms of the treaty outlined that Mexico would have to recognize the annexation of Texas. It defined the US-Mexican border as the Rio Grande, not the Nueces River. Mexico also had to sell all the territory north of the Rio Grande and California to the American government for $15 million.

The US came out of the war the clear winner and with an enormous chunk of land. The land it received was almost as big as Louisiana had been, and its acquisition changed the US completely. For Mexico, the war was disastrous, and the Mexicans came out of it with heavy losses and no gains.

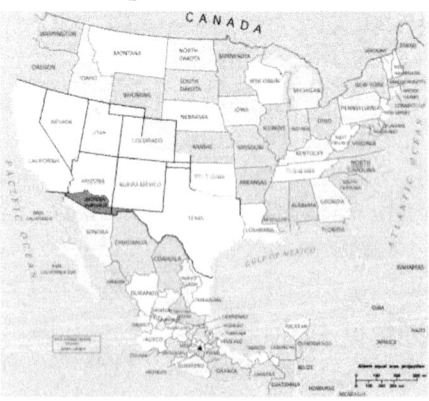

A look at what the US gained after the war. It received everything in white; the area in brown was contested by Mexico after the treaty.
https://commons.wikimedia.org/wiki/File:Mexican_Cession_in_Mexican_View.PNG

Northwestern Territory

The US had its eye on other parts of North America as well. The Pacific Northwest was a coveted tract of land that several countries competed for as early as the 18th century. Spain, Britain, Russia, and the United States all wanted the territory for themselves. It became even more important after the War of 1812 for diplomatic reasons. In 1825, both Russia and Spain signed treaties formally withdrawing their claims to the region, leaving the US and the British with contested control over the area.

An ongoing dispute ensued on who had sovereignty over a specific area of the Northwest Territory. For the British, the region was called the Columbia District, while the Americans called it Oregon Country.

In 1844, the Democratic Party suggested annexing the area. The Whig Party wasn't interested in the dispute, as it felt there were bigger issues to consider.

After some time, Polk offered the British a compromise, the 49th parallel, but the British refused. They wanted the border to be along the Columbia River.

After the offer was refused, Polk was advised to annex all of the Pacific Northwest, but tensions with Mexico over Texas were on the rise. Polk did not want to be in a situation where America would have to fight two wars simultaneously.

Treaty of Oregon

The US came to a compromise with the British and signed the Treaty of Oregon on June 15th, 1846. For nearly three decades, Britain and the United States had jointly occupied the Pacific Northwest. But with US resources stretched in the Mexican-American War, the Americans knew they had to settle the matter in the northwest to avoid fighting a war on two fronts.

The original proposal of the 49th parallel was established in the treaty as the border between the two countries. Those south of the 49th parallel would be American citizens, while those north would be British. Vancouver Island remained a British territory, while the San Juan Islands were left as a question mark that would be decided upon later.

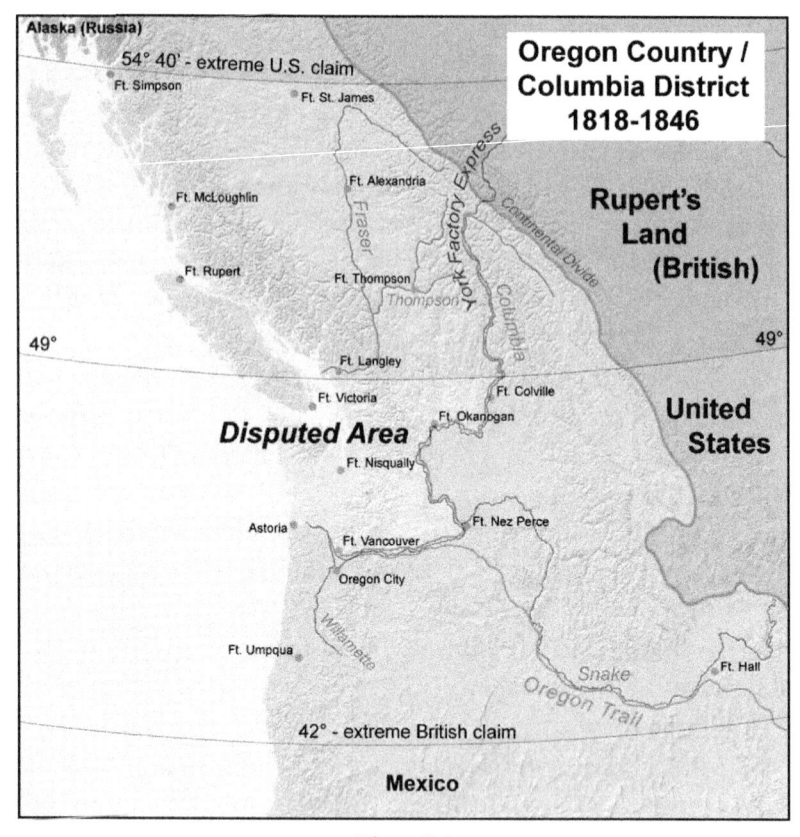

[Map: Oregon Country / Columbia District 1818-1846, showing Alaska (Russia), 54° 40' - extreme U.S. claim, Ft. Simpson, Ft. St. James, Ft. McLoughlin, Ft. Alexandria, Ft. Rupert, Ft. Thompson, Rupert's Land (British), 49° parallel, Ft. Langley, Ft. Victoria, Ft. Colville, Ft. Okanogan, Disputed Area, Ft. Nisqually, United States, Astoria, Ft. Vancouver, Ft. Nez Perce, Oregon City, Ft. Umpqua, Snake, Oregon Trail, Ft. Hall, 42° - extreme British claim, Mexico]

49th parallel.

Kmusser, CC BY-SA 2.5 <https://creativecommons.org/licenses/by-sa/2.5>, via Wikimedia Commons; https://commons.wikimedia.org/wiki/File:Oregoncountry.png

The treaty did not please Upper Canada, as the people there felt that Britain was not doing a good job of looking out for their interests or even taking their opinions into consideration. They were increasingly looking to have more independence, especially when it came to international matters.

California Gold Rush (1848-1855)

As the United States continued to expand, its population grew at a steady pace. Over the years, there would be waves of new immigrants, and the Gold Rush certainly led to such a wave. It was a hugely significant event in America's history and would shape the years to come, especially in the state of California.

In early 1848, a man named James Marshall, who was working in a mill owned by John Sutter, found flakes of gold in California.

They tried to keep the discovery quiet, but the word soon spread, sparking the Gold Rush.

People began to migrate there in masses, leading to a dramatic increase in the population of the country. In a matter of ten years (1850 to 1860), the number of people in California increased from 92,597 to 379,994!

Men and even some women gave up everything they had. They left behind families and gambled their life savings to try to score big in California. Known as the Forty-Niners, these hopeful gold miners arrived in droves in California, traveling on foot, on horses, and on boats.

Prospectors during the Gold Rush
https://commons.wikimedia.org/wiki/File:1850_Woman_and_Men_in_California_Gold_Rush.jpg

The gold that was easily accessible on the surface went fast, and by 1850, there was hardly any left, leaving people no choice but to start mining for it. Mining was expensive, so companies and rich individuals ran the enterprises and hired help.

Mining was difficult, dangerous, and laborious. Life for the people in mining camps was tough. The mining camps themselves were lawless and unruly. Crime, drinking, violence, and prostitution thrived there.

During the Gold Rush, over 750,000 pounds of gold were found. Thousands of people extracted $2 billion worth of gold, making some people very rich and changing their fortunes forever. However, for most, the Gold Rush led to nothing extra in their pockets. Some died or became destitute in California. Many ended up staying in California, shaping the state's history in ways that could not have been imagined prior to the Gold Rush.

Unfortunately for Mexico, the gold was discovered just a few days before the Treaty of Guadalupe Hidalgo was signed. It was of the utmost importance for the US that it gained control of California.

In late 1849, California applied to become a part of the United States. The application was quickly accepted in large part due to the discovery of gold and the huge population influx. California even skipped the step of becoming a territory! But the people in California had a caveat: they wanted to join as a free state. This caused a crisis in Congress, as slavery continued to be a contested issue.

The Compromise of 1850 saw California admitted as a free state. It also strengthened the fugitive slave laws and banned the slave trade in Washington, DC (although slavery itself was still allowed there).

California Genocide

While the Gold Rush meant riches and good fortune for many, for California's indigenous population, it was anything but. Their fairly peaceful existence was disrupted, and worse still, they were seen as a hindrance by white settlers. What would later become known as the California genocide is seen as one of the state's most heinous and shameful acts.

Soon after becoming a state, the government decided it needed more land to look for more gold and to make room for California's expanding population. To acquire the land, they needed to get rid of the Native American population, and the easiest way to do so was by killing them.

Fueled by bigotry and fear, the white settlers set out on a crusade to "exterminate the savages before they can labor much longer in the mines with security" with the government's blessing and support.[2]

Over a period of twenty years, over 80 percent of the indigenous population in California was eradicated through genocide. Tribal populations and villages were wiped out entirely through massacres.

A law was passed giving Americans the right to enslave Native Americans or take their children. White settlers were also given the authority to arrest the natives or force them into labor. While they were essentially still being kept as slaves, the acts allowed Americans to do it in a "legal" way. Children were often taken away and forced to attend schools to help them assimilate into white culture. The majority of these children never returned home.

It is estimated that of the 150,000 indigenous people who were in California at the start of the Gold Rush, 100,000 were killed in the first two years. Just over twenty years later, only thirty thousand indigenous people remained.

Today, California is one of the most diverse states in the United States and is home to 109 indigenous tribes. A formal apology was offered by the state in 2019 for the atrocities committed during the California genocide.

The Republican Party in 1854

Before we talk about the next major event in US history (the Civil War), it is important to talk about one more notable event that happened during the Gold Rush period: the formation of the Republican Party.

Up until the 1850s, the two dominant political parties were the Democrats and the Whigs. Former members of the Whig Party began to meet to discuss the possibility of creating a new party that opposed slavery. The breakdown of the party came about as a result of the admission of Kansas and Nebraska as states to the Union.

In January 1854, the Missouri Compromise (which set a boundary for which states could be slave states and which could be free) was repealed, and the Kansas-Nebraska Act was introduced.

---

[2] Blakemore, Erin. "California's Little-Known Genocide." https://www.history.com/news/californias-little-known-genocide.

Under this act, the tract of land to the west of Missouri would be divided into two territories, and they would be allowed to decide for themselves whether they wanted to keep or abolish slavery. Essentially, they could join as a free or slave state.

This did not sit well with those who were opposed to slavery because it opened up the door for slavery to exist in territories where it had previously been banned. The politicians who opposed slavery did so more out of fear of slave-owning states gaining all the power rather than morally opposing slavery. If the number of slave states dominated the number of free states, then politically, those states would get their way with the government and hold more power.

As the Whig Party fell apart over this controversy, anti-slavery Whigs continued to meet. On March 20th, 1854, they formed the Republican Party. They quickly gained a lot of support and played a hugely significant role during the American Civil War.

A Republican named Abraham Lincoln would go on to become president. He would be the one to formally abolish slavery in the Confederate States, which set the wheels in motion to abolish slavery in the entire US.

PART THREE:
The Civil War and the Reconstruction (1861–1877)

Chapter 10: What Caused the Civil War?

When the United States was just Thirteen Colonies, it was easy to find common ground and remain united. However, as the country expanded and as more territories joined, differing political views, values, morals, and goals began to cause tensions between the states.

One of the most glaring issues was the glaring economic differences between the North and the South. This, coupled with the continuing debate over slavery, led to increased friction.

By the middle of the 19th century, America was really starting to come into its own. It had defeated European empires, settled its conflicts with neighboring Mexico and Canada, and dramatically expanded its territory. Immigration was booming, and there was growth in almost every sector. However, there were key differences in how Northern states, like New York, and Southern states, like Georgia, made money.

In the North, the economy was driven by manufacturing and industries, and business was booming. The Northern states were rapidly becoming industrialized and enjoying wealth and prosperity, whereas economic growth in the South was less dramatic. In the Southern states, agriculture and farming were the main sources of income. Some people had rolling plantations and endless acres of land, which were used to grow cotton, tobacco, and other crops. But the majority of the South was made up of smaller farms. Of course, the backbreaking work was done almost entirely by black slaves. Plantation owners and even small farmers were dependent on slaves. They worried about what would happen to their source of income and their economy if slavery were abolished.

Early in 1854, the Kansas-Nebraska Act was passed by Congress, which essentially allowed these new territories to have slaves if they wished. This intensified the already heated issue and set off a series of events that ultimately culminated in the Civil War.

First, after the state of Kansas was created in 1854, battles between pro- and anti-slavery forces erupted in the territory and continued sporadically for the next five years. They were vicious, violent battles and became known as Bleeding Kansas.

The Dred Scott Case

The already tense political atmosphere worsened three years later when the Supreme Court handed a ruling in the Dred Scott case.

Dred Scott was a young man who had been born into slavery. When his master took him to a free state, he technically became free, but upon his return to a slave state, he once again became enslaved.

Scott sued for his freedom, arguing that once he had been freed, he could no longer legally be a slave. The courts disagreed, and in 1854, he appealed the decision to the Supreme Court. In 1857, the court ruled against him, and he lost his bid for freedom. The Supreme Court ruled that people with African ancestry could not claim citizenship. It has been labeled as one of the worst decisions the Supreme Court has ever made.

Dred Scott.
https://commons.wikimedia.org/wiki/File:Dred_Scott_photograph_(circa_1857).jpg

The decision seemed to support the Kansas-Nebraska Act. Abolitionists were furious at the decision, and anti-slavery sentiments increased and gained momentum.

Secession of States

In 1860, Abraham Lincoln, a Republican who was firmly against the practice of slavery, was elected as the sixteenth president of the United States. Even though Lincoln had made no plans to free the slaves because doing so would go against the Constitution, the Southern states decided they had had enough.

A convention was called in January 1861, and the delegates decided that South Carolina would secede from the United States. Six additional states also seceded: Florida, Georgia, Louisiana, Mississippi, Alabama, and Texas. Four other states—Tennessee, Arkansas, North Carolina, and Virginia—did the same later that year. Eventually, the group of eleven states would band together to become the Confederate States of America. During the Civil War, they would be known as the Confederacy, while those fighting for the North would be referred to as the Union.

Start of the War

Within a month of the initial states' secession, the states created a government and named Jefferson Davis as the interim president.

The Confederacy began to make moves almost immediately. President James Buchanan, who was leaving office in 1861, refused to surrender any of the Southern ports to them. Confederate troops retaliated by forcefully seizing them. A ship making its way to Fort Sumter with supplies for Federal forces was forced to turn around.

However, the war didn't officially start until Lincoln took office. When Lincoln was inaugurated, he reaffirmed that he had no intention of abolishing slavery in the slave states. He also refused to accept the secession and called for the country to unite and resolve its differences.

Meanwhile, Fort Sumter was still without supplies, so another attempt was made to deliver them. Lincoln hoped to avoid a confrontation, so he advised South Carolina beforehand. Robert Anderson, the man in charge of the fort, was asked to surrender. Anderson again refused to abandon Fort Sumter. On the following day, the militia commander, P. G. T. Beauregard, opened fire early in the morning, around 4:30 a.m., on Fort Sumter.

A few hours later, Abner Doubleday fired back, at which point Beauregard unleashed a barrage of shots, firing three thousand shots in a span of thirty-four hours. On April 13th, cannon fire pierced through the fortress, starting fires in the post. There were no casualties in this first battle, although some Union soldiers died when a cannon exploded in the fort while giving a salute on April 14th. Anderson finally agreed to evacuate the fort. The Civil War had begun.

Chapter 11: Key Battles and Campaigns of the Civil War

Before we delve deeper into the battles and campaigns of the Civil War, let's take a closer look at the opposing groups.

Union Army

Also known as the Federal Army, the Northern Army, or the Yankees, the Union included twenty states:

- New York
- Maine
- Vermont
- New Hampshire
- Connecticut
- Massachusetts
- Rhode Island
- Pennsylvania
- Ohio
- New Jersey
- Indiana
- Illinois
- Kansas

- Wisconsin
- Michigan
- Minnesota
- Iowa
- Nevada
- California
- Oregon

A picture of the Union Army; General George McClellan, who led the Peninsula Campaign, is to the right of the stump.
https://commons.wikimedia.org/wiki/File:GeorgeMcClellan1861a.jpg

The president of the Union was Abraham Lincoln. The Union was anti-slavery, although not everyone was fighting to ultimately abolish slavery. Many fought because they wanted to keep the Union intact.

It should also be noted that residents living in western Virginia didn't want to secede, so that portion of the state became a part of the Union as the state of West Virginia. Even though it was part of the Union, it didn't fight for the Union. It and four other slave states—Delaware, Maryland, Kentucky, and Missouri—were border states. They maintained a fairly neutral stance throughout the war. They were not as reliant on slave labor as the Southern states but believed leaving the Union was the wrong way to go about things. Many individuals from the border states fought in the war, with most of them fighting for the Union.

Confederate Army

The Confederate soldiers, sometimes referred to as Southerners or Rebels, came from the states that seceded from the United States. They were as follows:

- Texas
- Louisiana
- Arkansas
- Mississippi
- Tennessee
- Georgia
- Alabama
- Florida
- South and North Carolina
- Virginia

Jefferson Davis was the president of the Confederacy.

The Confederate Army planned to fight a defensive war. The Confederates felt confident the North wouldn't want to engage in a full-scale conflict and would agree to a compromise to avoid a prolonged war. Southerners also felt their way of living left them better prepared to be soldiers. They had some great military leaders and a cause worth dying for. A combination of these factors led them to arrogantly believe a war with the North would be short and quick; they also believed they would emerge as the victors.

One of the more important things the Union soldiers had going for them was the North's ability to manufacture and produce weapons. By the time the Civil War started, the North was rapidly growing in industrial strength. The Southern economy was based on farming and agriculture, which wasn't ideal for financing or planning a war. The South also had a much smaller population, which created a significant disadvantage in terms of raising taxes and funds to finance the war. A smaller population also meant that when they suffered losses on the battlefield, they had fewer people to replace the fallen soldiers.

The Union Navy was also much stronger and more capable than the Confederate Navy. When Southern ports were subjected to blockades by the Union, the South was unable to ship its cotton to foreign ports, which dramatically reduced its exporting capacity and affected the Confederacy financially.

In short, the Union Army was better placed to fight the war in almost every way. However, they failed to take into account the South was more passionate about the war's cause and knew the South's terrain better. Both sides expected a short war and a quick victory. What neither side anticipated was the tenacity and determination of their foe.

Confederate Army.
https://en.wikipedia.org/wiki/File:ConfederateArmyPhoto.jpg

American Civil War

First Battle of Bull Run – July 21st, 1861

The First Battle of Bull Run (also known as the Battle of First Manassas) was the first major full-scale battle of the Civil War. It was an eye-opening experience for the two sides, both of which had naively assumed the war would be over quickly and with limited casualties.

After the Civil War started in Fort Sumter, the Union forces felt confident they could win the war in short order. This led to a premature offensive in Virginia by around thirty-four thousand Union troops, which were led by General Irvin McDowell. Only about eighteen thousand took part in the fight.

When the Confederate Army found out about the advance, General Beauregard gathered around twenty-two thousand troops. General Joseph Johnston also joined him with an additional twelve thousand troops. Again, only about eighteen thousand took part in the battle.

By the morning of July 21st, both sides were ready for a battle. It started when three Union divisions crossed the Bull Run stream, driving back the Confederate troops to Henry House Hill.

But Beauregard had a strong defensive line, which fired and fought back from a concealed slope. A sudden charge by the Rebels (another name for the Confederates) down the hill broke McDowell's line, and the Union troops were forced to retreat.

This gave way to chaotic, unorganized fighting and bloodshed. Almost three thousand Union soldiers died, went missing, or were wounded. The Confederates had almost two thousand casualties. It was a horrifying thing for civilians and the troops to witness. Wealthy families from DC came to picnic and watch the battle, expecting an easy Union victory. They also had to retreat hastily when the battle did not go their way. It also left the government feeling uncertain about how to proceed. A war they thought would be easily won was now looking far more complicated.

The Civil War began on April 12th, 1861, when the Rebels fired shots at Fort Sumter. It ended on April 9th, 1865, with the Confederacy surrendering to the Union. Over the course of four years, it is estimated that between 620,000 and 750,000 soldiers lost their lives to the bloody and violent battles. This number doesn't account for the thousands of innocent civilians who died as a direct result of the war. Historians estimate that number to be around fifty thousand, although the actual number of casualties is likely quite higher.

However, the Civil War wasn't fought entirely in vain. By the end of the war, the country had been united once more, although tensions were still high. Slavery was also abolished for good by the end of 1865.

While the war featured thousands of battles, only around fifty were significant, with some of those battles being more defining than others. We will take a look at the biggest battles of the war; if you are interested in this time period (or any other time period in US history), we strongly encourage you to check out the references to learn more about what happened in greater detail.

The Battle of Antietam – September 17th, 1862

During the Maryland Campaign, the Union won the Battle of South Mountain, while the Confederates won the Battle of Harpers Ferry. Hoping to secure another win for the Confederates, General Robert E. Lee ordered his forces to converge near Antietam Creek. The topography of the area made it ideal for mounting a defense. Lee's troops went into position on September 15th and waited for the Union troops to arrive.

Union General George McClellan's troops arrived the following afternoon. He sent a corps across the creek, where they found some of Lee's troops. The two divisions fought, and the next morning, at dawn, the Union troops launched an attack. The two sides attacked back and forth, putting up a formidable fight.

By late afternoon, the Union troops had managed to push back the Confederates and claim victory. Even after the battle was over, minor skirmishes continued for another two days before Lee and his men fully withdrew. McClellan decided not to follow Lee, which made Lincoln question his abilities. Feeling unsure about McClellan, Lincoln decided to put the Army of the Potomac under the command of Major General Ambrose Burnside.

Antietam would become the bloodiest one-day battle in the country's history. The battle saw a staggering 22,717 casualties: 12,401 on the Union side and 10,316 on the Confederate side.

After this victory, President Lincoln signed the Emancipation Proclamation, which will be discussed in greater detail in Chapter 12.

The Battle of Fredericksburg – December 11th–December 15th, 1862

Nearly 200,000 men fought in the Battle of Fredericksburg, making it the battle with the highest number of troops. General Lee led the charge with 72,500 Confederate troops against General Burnside, who had 106,000 soldiers. This was one of the earliest major battles of the Civil War, and it ended in a great victory for the Confederates.

Even though Burnside and his troops had arrived in Falmouth, Virginia, by November, they didn't have the pontoons to cross the Rappahannock River. Bad weather and snow further delayed them.

The delay allowed Lee to prepare. He correctly predicted that Burnside would cross the river, so he stationed Rebel troops in defensive positions along the river. When the battle started on December 11th, with Union soldiers crossing into Fredericksburg, they were shot at by Confederate soldiers.

Things continued to go badly for the Union soldiers; they lost twice the number of men compared to the Confederates. On December 15th, Burnside's men retreated, and the Rebels claimed an incredible victory. The win provided a huge morale boost for the Southern states and was a devastating blow for the Union.

A second offensive against Lee was mounted in January 1863, but this, too, was a failure. After this, Burnside resigned from his post and was replaced by "Fighting" Joe Hooker.

The Battle of Chancellorsville – April 30th–May 6th, 1863

After the disastrous Battle of Fredericksburg, the Union Army was left shaken and disorganized. Burnside resigned, and Hooker took over. Hooker's first order of business was to train the troops. His goal was to capture Richmond, Virginia, which was the capital of the Confederacy.

Hooker's plan was simple. He would send two-thirds of his troops near Fredericksburg to trick Lee into thinking they were planning a frontal assault. In the meantime, he would take the rest of his troops across the Rappahannock River.

But Lee, who had thought ahead, also decided to divide his troops and was thus ready for Hooker's army when they arrived near Chancellorsville on May 1st, 1863. Lee decided to split his troops once again. Thomas "Stonewall" Jackson, one of Lee's most trusted generals, marched ahead with twenty-eight thousand troops to attack Hooker's right flank, which had been left exposed.

Jackson destroyed half the Union troops that day. Later that evening, as he and his men went exploring in the forest, a North Carolina regiment started shooting at them, thinking they were Union troops. Some of the bullets struck him, and he broke his arm, requiring his arm to be amputated. He contracted pneumonia and died on May 10th, 1863. The Confederacy hailed him as a war hero.

On May 6th, Hooker and his troops retreated to Washington. The Battle of Chancellorsville lasted a week and ended in a huge victory for the Confederates. Lee seemed nearly unstoppable.

The Battle of Gettysburg – July 1st–July 3rd, 1863

The seemingly unstoppable General Lee's series of victories ended at the Battle of Gettysburg, which is perhaps the most well-known battle of the Civil War. It would be the turning point in the war.

Fresh from his victory at Chancellorsville, Lee made the decision to cross into Union territory. A year ago, Lee had been forced to turn back from the North after a Union victory at Antietam, but he was ready to try again. He also hoped the invasion in the North would divert some Northern troops away from the ongoing siege of Vicksburg, which will be discussed shortly.

Lincoln was having difficulties finding the right commander for the Army of the Potomac. Mere days before the battle at Gettysburg, he appointed General George Meade. Meade's orders were to follow Lee and make sure Union troops prevented him from getting to Washington.

On June 15th, Lee led parts of his army across the Potomac, and by the end of the month, they had reached the Susquehanna River. The battle began on July 1st when a group of Confederate troops made their way to Gettysburg, Pennsylvania, for supplies. They were confronted by a Union cavalry unit, which held them off until more reinforcements arrived.

By the afternoon, the chance encounter at a road junction between the two forces had erupted into a ferocious battle. For three days, the Unions and Confederates continued to battle with heavy losses on both sides. An estimated 51,112 soldiers were killed: 23,049 from the Union side and 28,063 on the Confederate side.

The Battle of Gettysburg.
Adam Cuerden https://en.wikipedia.org/wiki/File:Thure_de_Thulstrup_-_L._Prang_and_Co._-_Battle_of_Gettysburg_-_Restoration_by_Adam_Cuerden.jpg

It was the bloodiest battle of the Civil War. When it became clear the Union Army was winning, Lee retreated and began to head south. Meade made the decision not to go after him, much to Lincoln's displeasure.

Feeling defeated, Lee tried to resign from his post but was refused by President Davis. Even though other battles would still be fought before the Civil War ended, Gettysburg was seen as the final decisive battle where the tide turned in favor of the Union. Gettysburg would be the last full-scale invasion in the North by Confederate troops. Lee's defeat essentially put an end to any hopes of the Confederate States becoming an independent nation.

Within a few months of the battle's end, the Gettysburg National Cemetery was established. On November 19th, 1863, Lincoln delivered his most famous address. In his speech, he highlighted the Civil War as no longer just a fight to preserve the Union. It was a fight for democracy, liberty, and equality. He pledged that the nation "shall have a new birth of freedom and that government of the people, by the people, for the people, shall not perish from the earth."[3]

Vicksburg Campaign – December 29th, 1862-July 4th, 1863

When the Civil War started, the Southern states had control of the Mississippi River, which was an important waterway for the country, as it provided a link to countries outside of the US. The Union would ultimately take control of the vital water route. Vicksburg would end up being a decisive and successful victory for the Union Army, but it would also be the longest campaign of the war.

During the winter of 1862/63, General Ulysses S. Grant tried to take the city, but his campaign was unsuccessful. He tried again in the spring of 1863. This time, he expected a long siege, so he had the army construct trenches to enclose Confederate soldiers, who were led by General John Pemberton.

Twenty-nine thousand troops were trapped within the perimeter, and in a matter of weeks, Vicksburg was captured by Grant and his men. Unsuccessful attempts were made by other Confederate troops to rescue the trapped force.

Pemberton put up a valiant effort and held out for nearly two months. On July 4th, a total of forty-seven days after the siege began, Pemberton finally surrendered to the Union. This defeat was a key event in the Civil War. After the Union Army successfully defeated the Rebels at Port Hudson in Louisiana, control of the Mississippi River was finally in their hands.

The Battle of Spotsylvania – May 8th-May 21st, 1864

After Gettysburg, a series of battles were fought in Virginia. General Ulysses Grant's main objective was to pursue Lee, defeat his army, and capture Richmond, the capital city of the Confederate states. He instructed General Meade and the Army of the Potomac to pursue Lee relentlessly. That pursuit led them toward

---

[6] "Battle of Gettysburg." https://www.history.com/topics/american-civil-war/battle-of-gettysburg#section_1

Spotsylvania; their goal was to get in between Richmond and Lee's army.

As both armies reached the area, they were determined to block the other's progress. A twelve-day battle ensued, with heavy casualties on both sides. Nearly 3,000 Union troops died during the battle, while an additional 15,400 were wounded, captured, or missing. The Confederate Army suffered fewer casualties, with approximately 1,500 dead and another 11,000 wounded or missing.

The end result of the battle remains inconclusive to this day, as both sides declared themselves to be the winners of the battle. The Confederate Army had maintained its defenses, and the Union Army had severely incapacitated Lee's army. Lee lost men he would not be able to replace.

Winner or not, it ended up being a significant and strategic victory for Grant because, little by little, Lee and his army were being run into a corner. He finally surrendered in April 1865 in Appomattox, Virginia.

The Battle of Atlanta – July 22nd, 1864

The Union Army's Atlanta Campaign started in May of 1864. The plan was for the Union Army to make its way from Tennessee into Atlanta, which was strategically important for the Confederate Army because it had a railroad and was a manufacturing hub. It was also close to Richmond, Virginia, which was the capital of the Confederacy.

Capturing Atlanta would be a significant victory. The battle started on July 22nd, 1864. The Union troops were led by Major General James McPherson and Major General William Tecumseh Sherman. During an engagement with Confederate troops, which were led by General John Hood, McPherson was shot and killed.

Unwilling to give up, the Union troops pressed on and continued to fight. They were able to successfully push back against the Confederate offensive, with the Confederates suffering heavy casualties, losing around 5,500 men (roughly 10 percent of their entire force).

Even though Hood and his troops retreated, they did not surrender. Sherman had managed to cut off Atlanta from the railroad to the east, but the Confederate troops held on tenaciously.

Sherman continued to shell the city and stationed his army near the west to cut off ties with the railroad there.

The city of Atlanta was successfully captured by Sherman and his men a few months later in September. Following the victory, Sherman and his men traveled out of the city and lay waste to the countryside of Georgia in a campaign that is now called Sherman's March to the Sea.

The march lasted from mid-November to December 21st, 1864. The troops traversed Georgia, pillaging and destroying everything they could get their hands on. They ended eventually surrounded Savannah, Georgia, and demanded its surrender. On December 21st, the mayor formally surrendered.

Native Americans in the Civil War

Nearly twenty thousand Native Americans fought in the Civil War. They chose sides based on their existing loyalties and what they believed in. They fought for their families, their sovereignty, and their tribes.

Many Native Americans wanted the status quo to remain (or for things to get better). Many also fought based on their beliefs about slavery. There were also tribes who were encouraged by wealthy Native Americans who owned slaves themselves to sign treaties with the Confederacy and fight on their behalf. Many tribes sided with the Confederacy, which promised to restore lands.

In the end, none of the Native Americans got what they wanted and instead ended up fighting each other, with nothing to gain from it.

End of the Civil War

The surrender came on the heels of the Battle of Appomattox Court House. By the early spring of 1865, the Confederate soldiers knew they were losing the battle. As the Rebels retreated westward, they were almost entirely surrounded by Union troops. However, unwilling to admit defeat, the Rebels, under Lee, mounted one last offensive on the morning of April 9th. But it quickly became clear to them that the Union soldiers far outnumbered them.

By late morning, without any food or supplies and facing a large number of Union troops, Lee made the difficult decision to surrender. Lee and Grant met at Wilmer McLean's home, where

Lee formally surrendered.

Although the war was over, it didn't put an immediate end to the battles, as news traveled slowly back then. After Lee surrendered, six other small battles took place. The last one, the Battle of Palmito Ranch, took place in mid-May. After this, the war was finally and truly over.

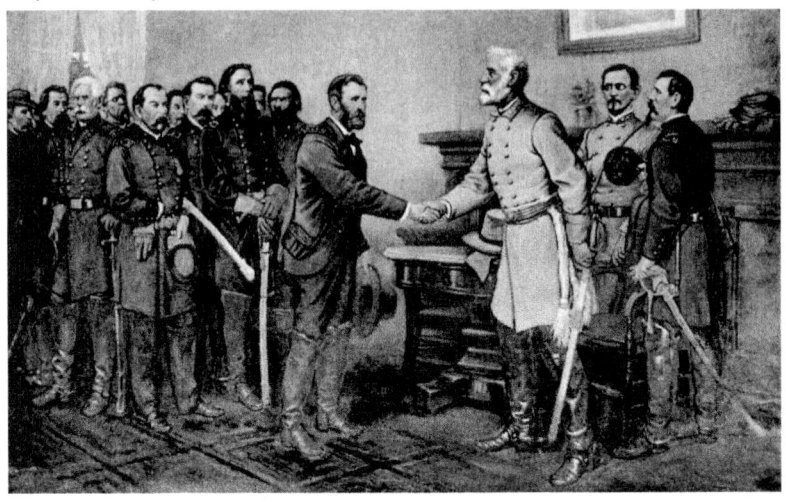

Painting of Lee's surrender to Grant.
https://commons.wikimedia.org/wiki/File:General_Robert_E._Lee_surrenders_at_Appomattox_Court_House_1865.jpg

Grant was very generous with Lee. He pardoned all the soldiers in the Confederate Army and allowed them to keep their private property, including their horses and sidearms. He even insisted on the Union soldiers sharing their food rations with the Rebels because, in his eyes, they were all Americans.

Chapter 12: Slavery, Emancipation, and the Aftermath

Slavery

From the country's earliest days, slavery had been a source of tension in the United States. as time went on, the divide between those who were for and against slavery deepened.

President Lincoln abhorred the idea of slavery, and he did not believe it had a place in the United States. However, he did not think he could abolish slavery completely since it would go against the constitutional right of slave states. He even says as much in his first inaugural address in 1861. Instead, he tried to educate the nation about it and tried to make sure any new states joining the country would not be allowed to establish slavery.

When the Civil War broke out, slavery was one of the reasons for the South's discontent. Lincoln himself stated the war was not about gaining freedom for slaves; the goal was to prevent the country from splintering into two.

As the war progressed and slaves began to flee from the South, some argued that if slaves in the South were freed, it would weaken the Confederate position since they were so reliant on slave labor. This would help the Union Army's war effort.

In July 1862, Congress decided that black men would be given permission to serve in the American forces. It was called the Militia Act. A second act, called the Confiscation Act, stated that any slaves who were captured from Confederate states or supporters would be given their freedom.

Lincoln appealed to the border states for help with emancipation, but they were not interested. Abolitionists urged him to take a firmer stance on slavery, but Lincoln didn't want to because his main priority was to bring the country back together.

Emancipation Proclamation

In the meantime, Lincoln's Cabinet was working on a document regarding slavery. Lincoln's secretary of state, William Seward, advised him to sit on the document and only release it after the Union Army won a big victory.

The victory came during the Battle of Antietam, where the Union forces crushed Lee and his troops. A few days later, Lincoln's document, which would become known as the Emancipation Proclamation, was announced. The proclamation implored the Confederate States to come back into the Union by January 1st, 1863. If they did not do so, then Lincoln vowed that all "persons held as slaves ... within the rebellious states ... are, and henceforward shall be free."[4]

When January 1st rolled around, the Emancipation Proclamation became law. In the past, when Lincoln encouraged emancipation, he had talked about providing compensation to slave owners or emigration for the slaves, but this was no longer his stance. He viewed the proclamation as a wartime measure.

Contrary to popular belief, Lincoln did not free all the slaves. The proclamation only applied to the slaves in Confederate States. Regardless, the Emancipation Proclamation created a foundation and set the stage for slavery to be permanently abolished. It also gave African Americans a stronger reason to win the war. It made the war a fight for freedom.

---

[4] "The Emancipation Proclamation." https://www.archives.gov/exhibits/featured-documents/emancipation-proclamation.

The goal of the Civil War began to shift. Although uniting the Union was still at the top of the agenda, abolition began to become more important. Perhaps it was hard for Northern politicians to imagine putting those who had been freed back into bondage. Congress and Lincoln began working on the Constitution to add an amendment that would abolish slavery.

At the end of January 1865, the Thirteenth Amendment was passed. It would not be ratified until December. Lincoln, who had been hesitant to take a firm stance on emancipation initially, declared in February 1865 that he hoped this would become his legacy. It is safe to say that it did.

Border States

Not all slave states left the Union to join the Confederacy. The five states that remained part of the United States included Kentucky, Maryland, Missouri, West Virginia, and Delaware. Throughout the Civil War, they were known as the border states.

At the start of the Civil War, most of the border states were neutral. Some individuals even sided with the Confederacy, as they felt that the North was being unfair toward them. But as the war continued, there was a shift in sentiments.

Kentucky was neutral at the start but shifted its stance to side with the North. Kentucky's support contributed greatly to the war effort for the Federalists.

The same was true for Maryland. It was strategically located between Virginia and Washington, DC. Had Maryland seceded, things may have gone very badly for the Union Army. In 1864, Maryland voted to abolish slavery.

While Missouri was officially neutral, a significant percentage of the population felt that the war against the Confederacy was wrong and sent soldiers to support them. As the war progressed, the state government divided into two: one was pro-Confederacy, while the other was pro-Union.

Delaware was loyal to the Union, and its loyalty did not waver during the Civil War.

Things were a little more complicated for West Virginia, as the Civil War was the catalyst that split Virginia into two. While West Virginia was a staunch Union supporter, many people did not agree and joined the war effort on the side of the Confederacy.

Even though, for the most part, the border states' governments did not engage in active fighting, they were strategic allies for the Union and helped the war effort by providing supplies, materials, and money. Individuals fought in the war, but they weren't sent by the state government. Geographically, their support was also important.

The neutrality of the border states is one of the reasons Lincoln was so hesitant to come down hard on slavery. He didn't want to alienate the border states that were still pro-slavery.

By the time the Civil War was in full swing, a significant majority of the people in the border states had sided with the Union troops. Approximately 275,000 men from the border states joined the war on the Union's side. The Confederate Army had much less support, with approximately seventy-one thousand men from the border states fighting for them.

Aftermath

Once the war was officially over, the country was left ravaged and war-torn, especially in the South. The Thirteenth Amendment of the Constitution, which was ratified in late 1865, further impacted the South, as it led to the abolishment of slavery across the country.

Approximately four million slaves became free. Over the next five years, former slaves were granted equal citizenship, as well as the right to vote. Unfortunately, President Lincoln, the man who had fought so hard for this moment, would never see it happen.

President Lincoln.
https://commons.wikimedia.org/wiki/File:Abraham_Lincoln_O-77_matte_collodion_print.jpg

The Assassination of President Lincoln

The man who pulled the country through the Civil War would not live to see the country united once more.

Even when Lee and his army surrendered, some Southerners firmly held on to the belief that they could still create a Confederate country if Lincoln was killed. A famous actor named John Wilkes Booth was a staunch supporter of the Confederacy. He hatched a plot to assassinate President Lincoln and his successors so the American government would be left without clear leadership or direction. And in that turmoil, the Confederacy could be restored.

On April 14th, 1865, five days after the Confederacy's surrender, President Lincoln was in his private box at Ford's Theatre, watching a performance of *Our American Cousin*. Booth waited for a moment when the audience would be laughing and shot the president in the back of his head. Lincoln died the following day.

No other important figure was assassinated, although there was an attempt on Seward's life. On April 26th, Union troops tracked down and tried to capture Booth. He ended up getting shot by a Union sergeant and died within a few hours. The men and one woman who conspired with Booth were arrested, convicted, and hung to death on July 7th, 1865.

Lincoln may not have lived to see the fruit of his labor, but his legacy would set the foundation for the country the United States would become.

Chapter 13: The Reconstruction (1865–1877)

American history is colorful and volatile. However, back in the mid-1850s, nothing had been as significant, brutal, or as impactful as the Civil War. The country was unified once more, although the process of formally admitting the Confederate States would take some time. The war also traumatized a generation, resulted in hundreds of thousands of lives lost, and created deep resentment.

Once the dust settled, the country was faced with a monumental task. The government had to rebuild the nation. The turbulent decade following the end of the Civil War became known as the Reconstruction. The country was in uncharted territory and found the period difficult to navigate. The Confederate States returned to the Union, and millions of freed slaves struggled to find their place in society.

Congressional Reconstruction

The Reconstruction Acts outlined the terms and conditions for the Confederate States to rejoin the Union. The bills were written in Congress by Radical Republicans and were enacted in 1867 and 1868.

After Lincoln's assassination, Vice President Andrew Johnson was sworn in as the seventeenth president of the United States. He wanted to unify the country, but as a Southerner and former slaveholder, he also didn't want to be too harsh with the Confederate States. His instincts told him to be laxer and more lenient with the South. The Radical Republicans were fiercely opposed to this approach. The anti-slavery group in Congress determined that freed slaves should be given equal rights, and they wanted stricter measures for the Confederate States.

After going back and forth, the Reconstruction Acts were created. A major point in one of the acts was the requirement to create five military districts in the South. For a rebel state to rejoin the Union, they also had to create and draft a new state constitution, which would need to be approved by Congress, and ratify the Thirteenth and Fourteenth Amendments (the Fourteenth Amendment granted citizenship to formerly enslaved people). President Johnson did not agree with these measures, but his concerns were overridden by Congress.

Beginning in 1868, the Confederate States began to come back into the Union. Georgia rejoined the same year but was quickly expelled for removing black people from its state legislature. Two years later, on July 15th, 1870, Georgia rejoined for a second time, and the United States was finally whole again.

The Black Codes

At President Johnson's urging, the Confederate States were granted amnesty. They were also allowed to establish their own governments. It stands to reason that these governments would do what was best for their people and stay true to their values and beliefs. And for these states, slavery was still important.

To them, slavery was a precious institution that generated a lot of money. The South had been built on slave labor, and now the South not only faced much damage from the war but also had to come up with a new way to rebuild its economy.

To prevent African Americans from climbing the political ladder and to essentially force them to work for little wages, they established laws called the black codes, which severely limited African Americans' ability to integrate into society. By creating laws that restricted their lives, the white politicians created a system where a freed slave's life was quite similar to their enslaved life.

Slaves in the South were "free" on paper, but opportunities and privileges enjoyed by white people were denied to them. Their freedom and liberties were severely restricted. In many ways, they were just as trapped as ever.

This was made possible as a result of a loophole in the Thirteenth Amendment, which stated that slavery was forbidden unless it was used as a punishment for a crime. This led to Southern states criminalizing normal activities that could then be used to imprison African Americans. While the codes varied based on the state, some common laws included things like prohibiting African Americans from loitering in areas or engaging in conversations as a large group. Being unemployed was also considered a crime.

Black people had to sign yearly contracts agreeing to receive the lowest pay possible. Anyone who refused to sign the contract or forgot could be arrested and forced to pay a fine. Of course, most black people barely had any money, so their only option was to pay off their debt by working on farms. Nobody was exempt, not even children. This vicious cycle ensured the former Confederate States still had their slaves; they just weren't labeled as such. Such acts enraged many in the Northern states.

In 1866, the Civil Rights Act was passed by Congress, which gave black people some more rights, such as being allowed to own property or rent. They were allowed to enter contracts and even sue someone. It was a good start, but it wasn't nearly enough.

Fourteenth and Fifteenth Amendments

Things got slightly better, at least on paper, with the ratification of the Fourteenth and Fifteenth Amendments.

Under the Fourteenth Amendment, which was adopted in 1868, African Americans were allowed to become citizens. In theory, citizenship meant they had the same rights, protections, and liberties as other American citizens. The Fifteenth Amendment was ratified two years later, in 1870. It entrenched voting rights for black men by prohibiting states from forbidding any male citizen from voting due to race.

Eventually, the Southern states repealed the black codes, but unfortunately, it didn't do much to improve their lives, especially once the Jim Crow laws were established. Systemic racism, hatred, and fear toward African Americans persisted and would continue to persist for decades, allowing white supremacist groups like the Ku Klux Klan to flourish.

Johnson's Impeachment

Johnson clashed heavily with Congress over the Reconstruction Acts. The Radical Republicans despised him, while Democrats in the South marked him as a traitor. Johnson did nothing to enforce the acts, even though they needed a strong hand to make sure they worked. He also frequently pardoned ex-Confederates and openly defied the government he served.

In 1867, the Tenure of Office Act was passed, even though Johnson tried to veto it (he vetoed twenty-nine pieces of legislation, with Congress overriding him fifteen times). The act was designed to curb presidential power by requiring the Senate's permission before the president could dismiss a government official.

Johnson ignored the act and suspended the secretary of war, a man named Edwin Stanton, who was openly supportive of the Radical Republicans. Ulysses S. Grant, the famed Union general, was nominated in his place. Congress overruled the suspension, and Grant resigned from the post, which increased the people's respect and admiration for him. But Johnson would not budge and dismissed Stanton again.

Congress finally had enough. On February 24th, 1868, the House of Representatives passed a measure to impeach him. After an eleven-week trial, he was saved from being thrown out of office by one vote. When his term ended, Ulysses S. Grant, a Republican candidate, won the election and took over the presidency.

Ulysses S. Grant's Laws

When Ulysses S. Grant ran for president in 1868, the Ku Klux Klan's terrorist activities were at their peak, and the nation's political climate was fraught with tension.

Protecting African American rights was one of his top priorities, but he also did not wish to throw the country into another civil war. When he became president, he was faced with an overwhelming task ahead of him, and he set about trying to create an America for all.

In 1870, the Fifteenth Amendment was ratified, granting African American men the right to vote. He also helped Congress pass a series of acts between 1870 and 1875. These acts were called the Force Acts, and their purpose was to protect the constitutional rights of Americans while guaranteeing the Fourteenth and Fifteenth Amendments for African Americans. Under the Force Acts, the federal government had the right to enforce penalties (including using the military) on any states or officials who interfered in a citizen's right to vote, register, or hold office.

The acts were instrumental in reining in the illegal activities of groups like the Ku Klux Klan. Even though not everyone agreed with his policies, Grant won the 1872 presidential election by a landslide. However, his priorities would shift during his second term from black rights to dealing with the Panic of 1873, when the stock market crashed and plunged the country into a financial crisis.

Even with his attention divided, Grant signed the Civil Rights Act in 1875, which affirmed that all men were equal before the law.

Grant fought the hardest for African Americans out of any other president in the 19th century. He ensured they were given rights and that those rights were protected. He also made it possible for black people to vote, own land, and be seen as equals in the eyes of the law.

However, this would not last. Democrats began to win again, taking back seats in Congress. The government's attention shifted to other issues the country was facing. After Reconstruction ended, the Jim Crow laws were passed in the South. Poll taxes and literacy tests were established, making it more difficult for blacks to vote. Since blacks couldn't vote, their voice wasn't heard on the issues that mattered to them. And since they didn't vote, they couldn't sit on juries. Schools and libraries were underfunded. Segregation was the law of the land, and it would remain so until the civil rights movement in the 1960s.

PART FOUR:
From Reconstruction to WWI (1877–1917)

Chapter 14: From Reconstruction to Expansion

During the last few decades of the 19th century, the United States again turned its attention toward expansion. It focused its expansion efforts on immigration and innovation and annexed places around the world.

Transcontinental Railway

The railroad first came to North America in 1827, and three years later, it started to provide passenger services. By 1831, mail was being carried on the rails.

Over the next few decades, railroads kept expanding. By 1860, trains were running on over thirty thousand miles of railroad in the United States, and in 1863, the ambitious plan to construct the first transcontinental railroad began. It took six years to complete, but when it was done, it transformed America.

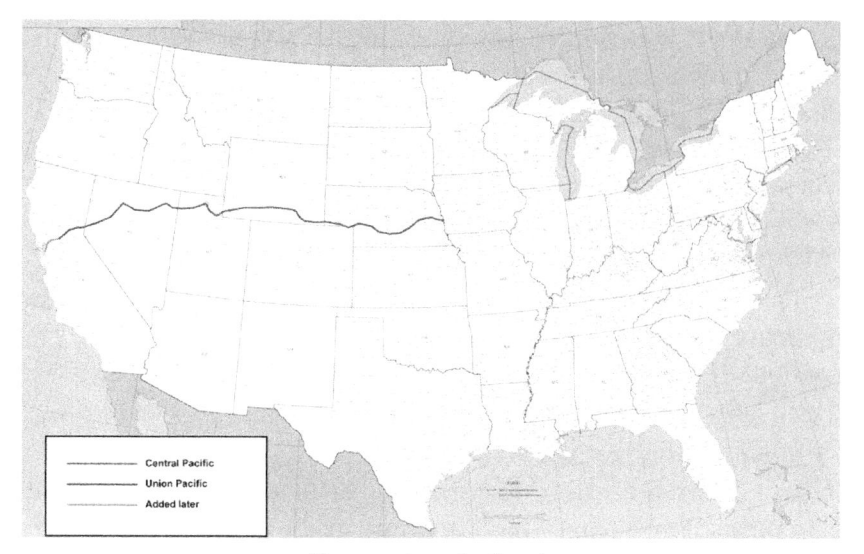

Transcontinental railroad.

Cave cattum, CC BY-SA 3.0 <http://creativecommons.org/licenses/by-sa/3.0/>, via Wikimedia Commons; https://commons.wikimedia.org/wiki/File:Transcontinental_railroad_route.png

The railroad connected the two American coasts. It made traveling more affordable and easier to export resources from one end of the country to the other. Before the transcontinental railroad, it would take nearly six months to go from New York to California and could cost $1,000 ($20,000 in today's money). After the railroad, the travel time was cut to just a week, and the cost was reduced to approximately $150 ($5,300 in today's dollars)!

The ease in transport allowed new businesses, such as mail order catalogs, to flourish and helped with the country's westward expansion, giving people more choices on where they wanted to live. As the country thrived, people in Europe began to look at North America with keen interest, leading to a period of mass migration.

The Industrial Age

The development of railways and other technological advances, such as the inventions of the telephone, electricity, the telegraph, and other things, dramatically changed the way people lived in America.

In Europe, many people were in search of a better life, as they had to deal with land shortages, lack of employment, and poor financial prospects. Many turned to America, hoping for a better life, and over a period of fifty years, from 1870 to 1920, more than eleven million immigrants arrived in the United States. Most of them were southern or eastern Europeans, but there was a significant wave of Chinese people who flocked to the country. Their cultures mixed with those already living in the country, leading to unique traditions. America certainly deserves its title of "Melting Pot."

The African American population also continued to grow, with many moving to the North. The number of immigrants may have continued to rise if not for the outbreak of the First World War, which led to a steep decline in immigration.

In addition to the war, the American government also started to make immigration more restrictive by setting limits on how many Europeans could come into America. In the mid-1920s, Congress passed a law barring all Asians from entering the country except for people from the Philippines.

Alaska

As the United States expanded, there was one tip of the continent that still remained beyond its control: Alaska. The US was keen to bring Alaska into the Union. Alaska would help the nation become a Pacific power, and the possibilities of finding gold or trading furs on a large scale were too tempting to pass up.

Russia was having a hard time managing the territory of Alaska due to the distance and lack of solid settlements. It was worried about losing the territory to Great Britain, so it was eager to sell the land to the US.

After a series of negotiations, Russia agreed to sell Alaska to the United States for $7.2 million. The purchase was finalized on March 30th, 1867. Some people refer to the purchase as Seward's Folly. Secretary of State William Seward pushed for the purchase so the country could gain a foothold in the Pacific. At approximately two cents an acre, most agree it was a good purchase. Alaska has many natural resources and adds to the grandeur of the United States.

Annexation of Hawaii

Ever since the original Thirteen Colonies had banded together to form the US, the government was more preoccupied with matters at home to really consider expanding internationally. By the time they started looking at conquering other lands, most of the world had already been divvied up, except for a few remote islands in the Pacific.

Hawaii was one such island, and the US wanted it. It had wanted the territory since the 1820s but couldn't do much about it. Hawaii had a monarchy, and the people were determined to keep the conquering European powers out of their island.

America gained entrance into Hawaii through the sugar trade. Sugar farmers (mainly white American men) in Hawaii were paid generously for their products. However, in 1890, the McKinley Tariff was approved by Congress. This raised the import rates of sugar coming from outside the US. Sugar growers realized that if Hawaii were annexed by the US, their tariff problems would disappear.

Around this time, Queen Liliuokalani came to sit on the throne. She was not fond of foreign powers interfering in island affairs, which would cause a clash between the two powers. When the sugar growers rose up against the monarchy in January 1893, US Marines were sent by the government to the island and forced the queen to abdicate.

It was up to Congress to figure out how to navigate these uncharted waters. Newly inaugurated President Grover Cleveland (who was serving his second term in office; so far, he is the only president to serve two non-consecutive terms) felt the Marines were in the wrong. He was an anti-imperialist and believed Hawaii should be left alone, even though the majority of the American population supported the annexation.

So, the matter was left in limbo until he left office. After the war with Spain started, Hawaii took on a new importance, as it could provide naval bases in the Pacific. President William McKinley signed a resolution to formally annex the islands. Hawaii became a territory in 1900, and in 1959, it became the fiftieth state of the US.

The Spanish-American War

While the United States was busy with railroads, immigration, and purchasing new territories, Spain was dealing with a rebellion from Cuba, whose people were striving for independence. This would be important for US history because it would lead to a war between Spain and the US.

The Cuban War of Independence and Spain's repressive measures and actions were covered extensively in American newspapers, leading to a lot of sympathy for the Cubans and their plight. The US government began to be pressured to intervene or do something, especially after the USS *Maine*, an American battleship, sank in Havana Harbor. The explosion was blamed on the Spanish, although it is believed there was something wrong with the ship.

Wishing to avoid conflict with the US, Spain announced its intentions to grant Cuba a limited form of self-government, but US Congress declared that Cuba had a right to become fully independent and insisted that Spanish forces leave the island. In retaliation, on April 24th, 1898, Spain declared war against America. The United States responded by declaring war on Spain the following day but making it retroactive to April 21st.

Two months later, American forces arrived in Cuba, and within a matter of days, they were engaged in the Battle of San Juan Hill, where the Spanish troops were soundly defeated. On July 3rd, 1898, the Spanish fleet on Santiago Bay in Cuba was destroyed by the Americans. A little over a month later, Spain formally surrendered.

Hostilities between Spain and the United States officially ended after the Protocol of Peace was signed on August 12th. The war itself came to a formal end on December 10th with the signing of the Treaty of Paris.

Under the terms of the treaty, Spain gave up any and all claims to Cuba, while Guam and Puerto Rico were ceded to the United States. Cuba would remain under American control until 1902 when the country gained its independence and became the Republic of Cuba. The exception was Guantanamo Bay, which had been seized by the Americans during the war with Spain to establish a naval base. A year after becoming a republic, Cuba agreed to let the US lease Guantanamo Bay and continue using it as a base. The US pays for the base every year, but only one payment has been cashed since Cuba's revolution in 1959.

Spain also agreed to accept $20 million from the US in exchange for transferring the sovereignty of the Philippines. This transfer of sovereignty would later turn into another headache for the US, as it led to another war. The US colonized the Philippines for forty-eight years. In 1946, the US formally recognized the Philippines as an independent nation.

But in the immediate aftermath of the Spanish-American War, the United States was feeling pretty victorious and powerful. It was rapidly emerging as a world power with interests and possessions beyond the North American continent. For Spain, losing the war meant its empire was on the decline.

Chapter 15: The Progressive Era

In the 17th century, America's focus was on expansion and building a strong, unified country. By the late 1890s, the country was pretty well established geographically and had enjoyed several decades of economic prosperity and industrial growth.

The bubble of prosperity broke with the Panic of 1893, and the economic depression ended in 1897. By this time, a wave of social activism was sweeping the country. This desire to create a better society became known as the Progressive Era.

Reformers had a vision of an equal and just society. They wanted to get rid of corrupt politicians and unfair or unethical practices. The movement had four aims:

- Protection of social welfare
- Moral improvement
- Creation of economic reform
- Foster efficiency

While industrialization had brought great prosperity to the country, there were many downsides as well, especially in how workers were treated and paid. Many businessmen had no issues with mistreating workers to increase their profits, and politicians did little to nothing to help the lower classes.

Reformers wanted better protections for people, as they believed that humans were capable of improving their conditions and environment. They also believed the government had a role to play to help make that happen. These beliefs slowly led to a shift toward more democratic and liberal values.

In this chapter, we will look at some of the most significant events to come out of an era that would be marked by a number of major reforms and social advancements around labor rights, economic reforms, women's suffrage, and racial inequalities.

First Labor Strikes

One of the earliest strikes to take place was the Great Railroad Strike of 1877. Workers were outraged when their wages were cut by the B&O (Baltimore and Ohio) Railroad. On July 14th, the workers began to protest, shutting down railroads in West Virginia and Pennsylvania. Over 100,000 workers protested in a number of cities and states.

Great Railroad Strike of 1877
https://commons.wikimedia.org/wiki/File:Harpers_8_11_1877_Blockade_of_Engines_at_Martinsburg_W_VA.jpg

With half the railroads shut down, state governors called on the militia to put an end to the uprisings. A total of one hundred protestors were killed, with another one thousand put in jail. The workers eventually went back to work. The strike did not lead to any big changes or accomplishments for them.

Coal mining in Pennsylvania started in the mid-1700s, and it quickly became an important part of the economy. The mines relied on hundreds of thousands of men and children. Child labor was one of the many things Progressives worked to fix. Child labor laws were put in place in 1938. Working conditions for miners were extremely dangerous, and the job itself was very hard. Miners did not get paid a lot and were often in a lot of debt. Yet the owners of the mine profited handsomely.

At some point, the workers had enough. On May 12th, 1902, the Coal Strike of 1902 began. Miners wanted better wages, more reasonable working hours, and their union to be recognized. It would be one of the most famous strikes of the Progressive Era. It lasted for a total of five months and deeply affected different sectors of the country. With each passing week, businesses, railroads, and factories started to run out of coal. Even schools and post offices threatened they would have to shut down. The lack of coal had a ripple effect, leading to price increases at restaurants, bakeries, hotel rooms, and even rents.

President Theodore Roosevelt was desperate to fix the situation but couldn't find a way to end the strike. He eventually reached out to J. P. Morgan, a wealthy businessman, who drafted a plan to end the strike. Roosevelt also created a commission to mediate problems and complaints between the miners and their employees.

According to the plan signed by both sides, the miners' workday was reduced to nine hours instead of ten. They were given a 10 percent increase in their salaries, which was retroactive. The employers did not recognize the union but stated their employees had the right to join unions.

This was a huge victory for the miners and spurred the American labor movement. It made workers feel they could make a difference in how they were treated and also showed businessmen that results could be achieved through peaceful negotiations. As the miners went back to work, things slowly went back to normal.

Another strike that had a significant impact on America was the Bread and Roses Strike. Workers at the Everett Mill in the town of Lawrence, Massachusetts, received their pay on January 11th, 1912. They were outraged to discover they had been paid $0.32 less.

The reduction was due to a new law in Massachusetts that cut back work hours from fifty-six to fifty-four hours per week, so employers decided to cut wages accordingly. The $0.32 was hugely significant since the workers made less than $9.00 a week.

The workers walked out, and the next day, workers in neighboring mills began to do the same. Utter chaos reigned, as strikers destroyed machine belts and bolts of clothing. They broke windows with bricks and inflicted other damages on the properties.

Within a day, over ten thousand workers were striking. Thousands more joined over the following weeks, demanding enough wages to give them food and dignity. Many of the banners read, "We want bread and roses, too," giving the strike its name.

Other American laborers had the strikers' backs. They collected money for them, handed out food, and were very supportive. But things became tense between strikers, their employers, and the police. Some parents were so worried that they sent their children away to Manhattan, relying on strangers to care for them.

When President William Howard Taft opened an investigation into the workers' claims, Congress was horrified to hear about the working conditions in the mills, the mistreatment of the workers, and how their life expectancy was dramatically reduced. Working conditions were poor in many other industries as well, such as the meat-packing industry and other factory jobs.

Eventually, the employers agreed to a 15 percent wage increase and overtime compensation. After nine weeks of striking, workers went back to work. This victory helped the Lawrence workers and also paved the way for workers in other industries to receive wage increases.

Many strikes took place in the US, but we can see in each of these examples what an important role the central government plays. It goes back to the reformers' belief that the government can help make lives better for the population.

Women's Suffrage Movement

While women's suffrage had begun in the 1820s, it became more prominent and visible during the Progressive Era. This was the period when women really started to come into their own. They became major leaders in pushing social and political movements forward. They were tired of being told their roles were at home; they wanted to make a difference.

Women's suffrage was a huge priority for many. They wanted the right to a better education and more employment opportunities. They also wanted the freedom to get involved in politics and, most importantly, to have their voices heard through the power of voting.

Even though each group gained some ground in its own way, a few groups felt they would be stronger as a united front. In 1890, two groups, the National Woman Suffrage Association and the American Woman Suffrage Association, joined together to form one group called the National American Woman Suffrage Association (NAWSA).

NWSA, or National Woman Suffrage Association.
https://commons.wikimedia.org/wiki/File:National_Women%27s_Suffrage_Association.jpg

The women in this group were no longer fighting to be given the same rights as men. Instead, they argued that women should be given the right to vote precisely because of how different they were. This approach helped their cause, as different groups saw how women's vote would aid their own political agenda. For example, advocates of temperance were keen to give women the vote because it would add a huge number of votes in their favor.

The fight for women's suffrage would come to a successful end on August 18th, 1920, when the Nineteenth Amendment was ratified. Under this amendment to the Constitution, women were given the right to vote.

Through the tireless work of reformers, American women were eventually allowed to own property and were given the right to control and manage their own money. They were allowed to have custody of their children in the event of a divorce. However, it took decades for all of these changes to take place. For instance, a woman could not have her own bank account until the 1960s.

In addition to getting the right to vote, women also pushed for prohibition and reforms in public health.

Progressivism in Black Communities

During the Progressive Era, the widespread activism and fight for social justice largely excluded black people. Even though they had been given certain rights after the Civil War, they continued to face discrimination, violence, and racial segregation.

The Jim Crow laws were in full effect by the 1920s. They made it illegal for a white person and a black person to marry. The laws made racial segregation legal, suppressed voter rights, and ensured black people remained oppressed.

In order to have their concerns heard, African Americans knew they had to fight against the racial injustice they faced on their own. With that in mind, white and black activists established the National Association for the Advancement of Colored People (NAACP) in 1909. Today, it is the oldest and largest civil rights organization in the United States. The NAACP worked tirelessly to raise awareness about the injustices faced by black people.

After William McKinley's assassination in 1901, Vice President Theodore Roosevelt took office. He strongly advocated for pro labor laws, fair trade, and reforms to fix racial inequalities.

Theodore Roosevelt.
https://commons.wikimedia.org/wiki/File:ROOSEVELT,_Theodore-President_(BEP_engraved_portrait)_(cropped).jpg

Roosevelt tried to bring more stability to black employees, who tended to be viewed as disposable by employers. They were typically the first ones to be cut from jobs or fired. Roosevelt also put changes in place to allow people to have equal opportunities for training and jobs, regardless of the color of their skin. When he was the governor of New York, he ended segregation in schools, allowing white and black children to be taught together.

His invitation to black civil rights activist Booker T. Washington to dine with him in the White House was met with stern disapproval and caused a lot of issues. Even though Roosevelt never did something like that again, these little acts helped break down some barriers.

Roosevelt's administration did not push for change as much as it could have due to strong resistance within the political system, but it did try to implement some things that served as stepping stones for African Americans in the decades to come as they continued to fight for equal rights.

Chapter 16: The Fate of the Native Americans

As the United States welcomed hordes of immigrants and continued to develop as a nation, you might be wondering what happened to the original settlers of the land. Violence and conflicts between the settlers and the Native Americans had been a constant problem since the early period of colonization. White settlers were determined to seize the land, as they needed it to expand and for its resources. They did so through treaties, trickery, trade, and violence.

Although this chapter will step back in time a bit, it is important to discuss what the Native Americans endured and how Progressivism failed to take them into account.

Indian Removal Act

When America was expanding, it needed the land that was being used by the tribes, as sharing seemed out of the question due to tensions between the settlers and the native population, who saw the ownership of land differently than the settlers. But in order to get the land, the US needed to remove the Native Americans living there.

The American government came up with the idea of the Native American reservation system in 1786. Under this system, indigenous people would be given land to live on, and they could continue to self-govern and live life under their own social traditions and cultural beliefs. Each tribe would remain its own independent tribe.

For nearly one hundred years, this system stayed in place and provided some form of balance. This isn't to say the conflicts ceased. There were a lot of problems with the reservation system. Brutality against the Native Americans continued, and land remained a source of tension.

Andrew Jackson was very keen on removing the Native Americans even before he became president in 1829. In 1814, he led troops against the Creek nation. After defeating them, approximately twenty-two million acres of Native American land was taken by the states of Georgia and Alabama.

President Andrew Jackson.
https://commons.wikimedia.org/wiki/File:Andrew_jackson_head.jpg

More land was taken by the government in 1818 after Jackson invaded Spanish Florida. The government did not send Jackson there with the implicit purpose of invading, but it did not do much to stop him. Jackson continued in this fashion until 1824, playing a key role in negotiating treaties with the natives for land in the east and trading it for lands in the west. For the most part, the indigenous population agreed to these treaties because they wanted to maintain the peace.

Tensions over land increased when the Supreme Court made a ruling in 1823, saying that while Native Americans could live on the land they occupied, they could never own it because America's "right of discovery" trumped their rights.

Five Native American nations—the Creeks, Cherokee, Chickasaws, Choctaws, and Seminoles—did their best to resist, but they eventually assimilated by learning how to farm in the European style and receiving a Western education. They became known as the "Five Civilized Tribes."

Realizing that something needed to be done, the government created the Office of Indian Affairs in 1824 to settle land disputes. Six years later, the Indian Removal Act of 1830 was implemented as a way of forcing the indigenous people off the coveted lands. They would be moved westward to lands in Oklahoma that weren't as desirable. Over forty-six thousand indigenous people were forced out of their lands. Numerous events, like the Mexican-American War and other conflicts, also hastened the removal of Native Americans from their land.

In 1851, the Indian Appropriations Act was created. This authorized the creation of reservations in several states across the country. According to the US government, the reservations would keep the natives off the desired land and leave it available for white settlers. Additional acts would be passed by Congress under the same name, which we will discuss further later in this chapter.

Conflicts and Wars

Unsurprisingly, Native Americans did not like the idea of reservations, although some moved there with little to no violent resistance. Escalating tensions between natives and settlers led to a series of battles and wars. The two sides had been engaged in conflict for centuries, so this section will focus on significant battles from the mid- to late 19th century.

Dakota War (1862)

The Dakota War, also referred to as the Sioux or Dakota Uprising, began on August 17th, 1862. It took place in southwest Minnesota along the Minnesota River.

A series of treaties between the Dakota and the government, which were signed from the early 1800s to 1858, considerably reduced the amount of land held by the Dakota tribe. To make matters worse, the US government violated the treaty agreements, made late payments, or paid the money directly to traders who claimed that the tribes had debts.

The Dakota went hungry, and the lack of income and other treaty violations increased their hardships. When the payment was yet again delayed during the summer of 1862, Dakota warriors were determined to retaliate and did so by killing five white settlers. The warriors then visited Chief Little Crow and asked him to lead them into battle so they could get back their land. Reluctantly, Chief Little Crow agreed. The following day, an attack was made on the Lower Sioux Agency. Attacks on settlements continued along the Minnesota River Valley.

The war had officially begun.

Sometime in August, Henry Sibley was appointed to command a troop against the Dakota. This would prove to be very hard for Sibley because of his intimate familiarity with the Dakota. He had known them for decades; he spoke their language, was friends with Chief Little Crow, and even had a Dakota child. But he did as he was told and took his troops into battle.

For five weeks, the two sides fought fiercely. When the US troops soundly defeated the Dakota on September 23rd, 1862, at the Battle of Wood Lake, it was a devastating blow for the tribe. Three days after this defeat, the tribe surrendered to the government.

While the war was over and the fighting had stopped, the men who surrendered were held captive to await a military trial. Non-combatant Dakota were forcefully removed by US troops and taken to Fort Snelling. The first groups arrived at the fort on November 13th and were placed temporarily on the river bottom beneath the fort while the soldiers began to build a concentration camp.

A wooden stockade was used to close off three acres of land. Approximately 1,600 Dakota people, mostly women, children, and the elderly, were moved inside the camp. Their movements were controlled by the guards stationed outside. That winter, several hundred Dakota people died. The prisoners were treated harshly by the Americans. They were abused, tortured, and tormented.

Several months later, in February 1863, Congress decided to annul all its treaties with the Dakota, with all the land and any annuities going to the US government. A month later, a second bill was passed to remove the Dakota people. In May, the remaining Dakota were taken away to a reservation in a desolate part of what is now South Dakota.

By the time the war came to a full end, the Americans had managed to wipe out most of the Dakota from Minnesota.

The Colorado War (1863-1865)

The Colorado War was fought between the Cheyenne and Arapaho tribes against the white settlers for control of the Great Plains in eastern Colorado. The territory rightfully belonged to the Native Americans under the terms of the Fort Laramie Treaty of 1851. However, as waves of new immigrants arrived in the area to settle and as miners began searching for gold, the need for resources and land increased.

At first, the tribes tried to resolve the matter peacefully. They even accepted a new settlement where the indigenous people gave up most of their land in exchange for a reservation and annuity. But it became difficult for the tribes to live off just the reservation, and the government payments and the tension from the Civil War made things worse.

John Evans, the governor of Colorado, wanted to keep the Native Americans away from white communities. He announced that all Native Americans who wanted peace should move closer to military posts to show they were not hostile. The tribes did as they were told, believing themselves to be secure. However, a few months later, on November 29th, 1864, Colonel John Chivington, with the support of Evans, marched his seven hundred men into the Sand Creek area and launched a surprise attack on the peaceful Native Americans.

Women, children, and men were hunted down and killed. Over 148 Cheyenne and Arapaho died, most of them children and women. Volunteers from Colorado went back to the village and made sure to kill the wounded before setting the village on fire.

The massacre was so brutal and atrocious that it led to a public outcry. Once the Civil War ended, the government tried to deal with the tribes in a less horrendous way. The Native Americans involved in this war had had enough. They moved northward, raiding forts and attacking the US forces they came across.

Texas-Indian Wars (1820-1875)

Conflicts with Native Americans had been a long-standing issue in Texas ever since the first Spanish and European settlers moved into the area. As Texas became a part of Mexico, then a republic, and then part of the Union, the conflicts and tensions with the natives continued. Things became particularly tense after the Mexicans left because, as we have seen, the US government was opposed to tribes settling in what it now considered to be its territory.

A series of battles took place from 1820 to 1875 and became known as the Texas-Indian Wars. The Comanche tribe was less concerned with maintaining peace than tribes like the Sioux. This meant the battles were bloody and violent.

One event of particular significance is the Salt Creek massacre, also referred to as the Warren Wagon Train raid. On May 18th, 1871, in the Loving Valley near Graham, Texas, a wagon train was making its way to a fort with supplies. A group of 150 Kiowa was hidden behind a hill, waiting for the wagon train to cross so they could raid it. During the raid, seven men were murdered.

After the successful raid, the natives thought nothing more of it, but for the Texans, this raid would be the straw that broke the camel's back. When the raid was reported to General William Tecumseh Sherman, who had led the March to the Sea during the Civil War and who was inspecting the military outposts of Texas at the time, he began to understand the fear under which Texans lived. Sherman ordered that the tribe's chiefs be arrested.

One chief, Satank, was killed while trying to escape, while the other two, Satanta and Big Tree, were arrested, tried, and sentenced to death. The governor of Texas, Edmund Davis, decided to give them life in prison instead. Chief Lone Wolf eventually negotiated an early release for them on the promise of good behavior. Neither one kept this promise. Satanta committed suicide in 1874 after getting captured, while Big Tree lived a life of confinement at Fort Sill. When he was released, he lived on a reservation and died in 1929.

By 1875, all of the original Native American tribes in Texas had been wiped out or forced to relocate. The Texas-Indian Wars formally ended when the last band of Comanche, led by a Quahadi warrior, surrendered and relocated to the Fort Sill reservation.

Today, Texas has almost no Native American land.

Great Sioux War (1876-1877)

As the conflict in Texas was coming to an end, another was simmering in Montana and Wyoming.

Between 1876 and 1877, the Lakota, Sioux, and Northern Cheyenne fought with US troops. Settlers tried to encroach on and seize their lands after gold was discovered in the Black Hills.

Once the gold was discovered, the US government wanted the land, which went against the terms of the Treaty of Fort Laramie of 1868. Under this treaty, the Sioux had exclusive rights to a portion of the territory, which included the Black Hills area. It also gave them land to be used for hunting. But after the discovery of gold, Americans began rushing to the Black Hills area, and there was nothing the government could do to stop them.

In 1875, a group of Sioux went to meet President Ulysses S. Grant. They requested that he honor their treaties and stop the miners. Grant suggested paying the tribes for the land and helping them relocate to Indian Territory. This was unacceptable to the Sioux. The series of battles that ensued is known as the Great Sioux War or the Black Hills War.

An important battle during this war was the Battle of the Little Bighorn. Fought near the Little Bighorn River, this battle was a decisive victory for the Native Americans. When George Custer's 7th Cavalry was tasked with scouting the area for enemies, they made their way to the Little Bighorn Valley. The Native Americans rallied together, and Custer's seven hundred men were met with over two thousand Native Americans. Custer himself commanded about 210 US troops; every man who fought with Custer died. The two messengers he sent out earlier were the only survivors of his unit. While it was a victory for the Native Americans, the killings further cemented the image white settlers had of natives being vicious and violent.

While battles were being fought, efforts were being made to resolve the matter through diplomacy. Congress stopped providing rations to the Sioux until they agreed to cede the land. The tribes began to divide, and in the spring of 1877, some groups began to surrender to the US.

However, Chief Sitting Bull, a Hunkpapa Lakota (also known as the Teton Sioux), refused to surrender. He led a group of Sioux to Canada, but in the summer of 1881, they came back. With no other options, they surrendered. The Black Hills was ceded to the American government.

Wounded Knee Massacre

One of the final events of the Sioux Wars took place at Wounded Knee, where a group of natives practiced the Ghost Dance. They believed that if they did the Ghost Dance and turned away from the white settlers' way of life, their gods would create a fresh world and destroy the enemy.

The Americans stationed there did not feel comfortable with such beliefs. On December 29th, a cavalry of American troops surrounded Ghost Dancers near Wounded Knee Creek. The US troops were worried the Ghost Dance meant the natives were going to attack. So, on that morning in December, they confiscated the natives' weapons. It is believed that a deaf Lakota man refused to surrender his gun. It went off, and the US troops started to attack. The Native Americans attacked to defend themselves, but they didn't have their guns.

The American troops slaughtered the natives. It is believed that between two hundred and three hundred Lakota died, most of them civilians. On the American side, thirty-one men died. Back then, it was called a battle, but today, we refer to this event as a massacre.

After the end of all the wars, the American government got what it wanted. It was successful in its attempts to remove and relocate the majority of the indigenous people onto established reservations.

Indian Appropriations Acts

As part of the "Indian problem," Congress passed a series of acts called the Indian Appropriation Acts. The first one, passed in 1851, established the creation of the reservation system and allowed the government to send the indigenous people to reservations. The act passed in 1871 stated that the US would no longer recognize indigenous people as members of a sovereign nation. Thus, the government no longer had to work on treaties with them. In 1885, the Indian Appropriations Act stated that tribes could negotiate the sale of land that was not occupied by anyone.

The Dawes Act

The Dawes Act of 1887 brought yet another dramatic change for the Native Americans. Under this act, the federal government broke up the lands given to the tribes into smaller plots. The tribes or people who accepted the plot of land would have the right to become US citizens.

The end goal of the act was to eradicate Native American cultural practices and traditions. The government's point of view was that the best way of solving the continued indigenous dilemma was to "convert" them into Americans. Politicians wanted to assimilate the natives into American society and "civilize" them.

After the Dawes Act went into effect, over ninety million acres of tribal land were taken away from the indigenous people and purchased by settlers. The Dawes Act ended when President Franklin Roosevelt's administration drafted the US Indian Reorganization Act in the 1930s. The new act allowed Native Americans to form their own government and stopped the parceling of land.

In June 1924, President Calvin Coolidge signed the Indian Citizenship Act, which granted all Native Americans citizenship to the United States. However, they were not granted full citizenship rights until the late 1940s.

The reformers wanted the Native Americans to be treated better by society, and they felt the best way of accomplishing this was to integrate them into American culture. They discouraged tribal landholding and encouraged Native Americans to give up their traditional way of living to adopt the American way. While some Native Americans were amenable to assimilation, others were less keen and resisted.

Chapter 17: Political and Economic Changes

Constitutional Changes

The Progressive Era saw more involvement from the government with regard to societal issues. The push for progress saw the establishment of several constitutional reforms and changes designed to make society fairer and more equal. The reforms also improved the life of the general public.

Three constitutional changes stand out during this time period.

Sixteenth Amendment

Present-day laws regarding paying federal income tax began with the ratification of the Sixteenth Amendment.

Under Article 1, Section 8 of the Constitution, Congress is authorized to collect taxes on income from American citizens. That money would be used by the federal government for the upkeep of the country for things like building bridges, maintaining the armed forces, enforcing laws, and other things.

The amendment was passed in Congress on July 2nd, 1909, and was ratified on February 3rd, 1913.

Seventeenth Amendment

In 1912, a change was proposed to Article 1, Section 3 of the Constitution, which allowed senators to be appointed by state legislatures. Under the amendment, people would be allowed to vote directly for American senators in each state.

The amendment passed Congress on May 13th, 1912. It was ratified almost a year later, on April 8th, 1913. This reform was seen as a solution to the electoral process, which was increasingly seen by the public as corrupt and ineffective. The amendment also ensured that big businesses, industrialists, and other wealthy people could not influence the process of selecting senators.

Nineteenth Amendment

The Nineteenth Amendment was a significant piece of legislation, as it finally gave women the right to vote. It was a hard-won victory for women suffragists, who had been fighting for it for nearly one hundred years.

It was approved in Congress on June 4th, 1919, and adopted into the Constitution on August 26th, 1920. It was the first step toward political equality for women and helped shift the mindset on what a woman's role was supposed to be. The 20th century is when women really started to come into their own, as they started to play a far more active role in American society. The traditional roles evolved, and women began to work outside the home, have careers, receive a formal education, and enter politics, although the changes didn't occur immediately after the Nineteenth Amendment passed. Regardless, this was a hugely historic moment for American women.

Presidents

As we've seen, the government played a more central role during the Progressive Era, as many reforms were pushed by the administrations of the sitting president. Three American presidents were viewed as being more progressive, and they played a significant role in pushing forward progressive reforms. They were Theodore Roosevelt, William Howard Taft, and Woodrow Wilson.

President Theodore Roosevelt

When President William McKinley was inaugurated on March 4th, 1897, he came to the White House with Theodore Roosevelt as his vice president. On September 14th, 1901, he died of gangrene caused by wounds sustained from an assassin's bullet. Roosevelt became president; he was the youngest man to serve as president.

Theodore Roosevelt believed that governments had a role to play when it came to the public's welfare, society's progress, and keeping businesses under control, just like the progressive reformers. And he was keen on implementing some meaningful changes.

For instance, Roosevelt was responsible for the Square Deal, one of the most important and influential policies of the 20th century. The domestic policy was geared toward helping the middle class and had three key goals:
- Protecting the consumer
- Controlling large corporations
- Conserving natural resources

He had a reputation as a "trust-buster," and during his time in office, his administration filed forty-four antitrust actions against some of the biggest corporations in the country. He was strongly supportive of regulating corporations, as he believed it would ultimately benefit the public at large. The regulations he passed ensured that the rights of both the consumer and the business were protected.

The Square Deal led to the establishment of several important acts and policies that continue to influence America today. Some of these include the Pure Food and Drug Act of 1906, the Meat Inspection Act, the National Child Labor Committee, and the Antiquities Act. Each of these acts was designed to safeguard the consumer.

A lover of nature, Roosevelt saw the need to protect and preserve nature. He was the first president who worked to conserve the country's natural resources. He worked hard to cherish and promote the vast, natural beauty of the United States. His preservation efforts included establishing 150 national forests, several national parks, game preserves, and national monuments.

Theodore Roosevelt's legacy continues to live on today.

President William Howard Taft

Once Roosevelt's presidency ended, William Howard Taft, a man whom Roosevelt had handpicked to replace him as the Republican presidential candidate, won the election.

Taft became president in 1909 and continued a lot of the work that Roosevelt had started. He filed nearly ninety antitrust actions and developed the Mann-Elkins Act, which gave the Interstate Commerce Commission (ICC) the authority to regulate phones, telegraphs, and cable companies. The act also put an end to railroad companies giving away free tickets or reduced fares to employees and their families.

Taft was a big supporter of the Sixteenth and Seventeenth Amendments and helped to create the Federal Children's Bureau and the Bureau of Mines, an agency dedicated to setting safety standards for miners.

Through the course of his presidency, Taft began to lose support within his party. Roosevelt considered running again, but ultimately the Republicans stuck with Taft as their candidate. Roosevelt created the Progressive Party with his supporters. Neither man won.

President Woodrow Wilson

The Democrats chose Woodrow Wilson as their nominee for the 1912 presidential election.

President Woodrow Wilson.
https://commons.wikimedia.org/wiki/File:Thomas_Woodrow_Wilson,_Harris_%26_Ewing_bw_photo_portrait,_1919_(cropped).jpg

Because the Republican vote was split between those who supported Taft and those who wanted Roosevelt, Wilson swooped in with the largest electoral majority seen in any presidential elections until that point.

Wilson's presidency was significant for a number of reasons. The last time Democrats had been in power was during the Civil War, and now they suddenly had power in the White House and both houses of Congress.

One of Wilson's campaign promises was around tariff and banking reforms. He put together an economic reform package called the New Freedom. The agenda dealt with issues involving tariffs, labor reforms, and banking. It went through Congress in late 1913.

The New Freedom plan introduced the concept of a federal income tax for the first time and outlined banking regulations, tariff reductions, and antitrust legislation.

But by 1914, Wilson's attention was on other things happening in Europe. The First World War had begun.

Wilson was determined that America's role in the global conflict would be as a peacemaker. He wanted the US to remain neutral and stay out of the war. The neutral position lasted until December 1917, when the US formally declared war on Austria-Hungary. Germany had started to engage in submarine attacks, and the US became the unwitting victim. Wilson felt the US had to enter the war in order to "make the world safe for democracy."[5]

Panama Canal Construction

One of America's goals throughout the 1800s was the construction of a trans-isthmian canal. They recognized that constructing a waterway between the Atlantic and Pacific Oceans would allow them to move ships and goods quickly and efficiently, which would lead to increased business.

---

[5] "Woodrow Wilson." https://www.whitehouse.gov/about-the-white-house/presidents/woodrow-wilson/.

In 1880, the man who built the Suez Canal in Egypt, Count Ferdinand de Lesseps, decided to tackle the project that would come to be known as the Panama Canal. The company quickly realized this would not be an easy task. Environmental factors like heavy rains and landslides and illnesses like malaria kept delaying the project. De Lesseps came to the conclusion that building a canal at sea level was too challenging and hard, so the project came to an abrupt end in 1888.

In 1902, the US, under the guidance of President Theodore Roosevelt, bought the French equipment and resources for $40 million and approached Colombia for the right to build on its territory. Colombia turned the US down, so the US helped the Panamanians with their fight for independence from Colombia. In November 1903, it formally recognized the Republic of Panama.

Following Panama's independence, the American government signed the Hay-Bunau-Varilla Treaty with Panama to get exclusive rights to the canal zone they needed. In exchange, the US gave Panama $10 million. It also agreed to pay an annuity of $250,000, which would start being paid nine years later.

The US formally began work on the canal in the spring of 1904 and almost immediately began to come up against much of the same obstacles faced by the French. The following year, John Stevens, a railroad specialist, was put in charge of the project. He implemented some changes right away, such as finding more efficient ways of doing the work and hiring West Indian people to work on the canal.

The working conditions for the workers building the Panama Canal were horrific and far from ideal. Canal workers made around twenty cents an hour, and their day was filled with hardships. If the backbreaking work wasn't bad enough, they were subjected to racial tensions and abuse. They also lived in constant fear of contracting a life-threatening disease, such as yellow fever or malaria.

They also had to work in a rough environment and deal with the changing weather conditions. Machinery accidents were common. A combination of all these factors resulted in daily deaths. It is estimated that around twenty-five thousand workers were killed during the construction of the canal.

A drawing of the Panama Canal
https://commons.wikimedia.org/wiki/File:The_Panama_Canal_-_The_Great_Culebra_Cut.jpg

Stevens also suggested constructing a lock canal as a workaround to the issue of landslides. A lock canal would allow ships to be raised to the level of the oceans before being lowered back down to the sea level.

William Gorga, the chief sanitary officer, also played an important role by systemically wiping out all the mosquitos in the area with crude oil and kerosene. This helped eliminate some of the diseases the workers suffered from.

Construction began in November 1906 and faced a few setbacks, such as Stevens resigning from the project and construction having to cut through mountains, but the obstacles were overcome. The project was completed in 1913.

On August 15th, 1914, the Panama Canal was officially opened. A grand celebration had been planned for the opening to showcase America's exceptional power and ability to do the impossible. However, due to World War I, the celebrations were scaled back.

In the end, the project cost the American government over $350 million and required over forty thousand laborers. Many of them died. The estimated number of deaths is 5,600, but historians believe the actual number is much higher. Thousands more sustained permanent injuries and were left crippled or disabled.

What did the Panama Canal do for America? Well, it made the nation one of the most powerful nations in the world because it had control over where two oceans meet. It also saved American ships a lot of money and time and generated new businesses because ships were able to move more quickly.

The Rise of Industrialists and Bankers

The Progressive Era wouldn't have been what it was without the influence of the industrialists and bankers.

Once the Civil War ended, the US went through the Reconstruction. When the dust settled, the country went through rapid industrial growth. New industries, such as steel manufacturing, petroleum, electricity, and many others, emerged while existing industries expanded and grew. Railroads, especially the transcontinental railway, transformed society.

In this period of enormous growth and expansion, a new social class emerged: industrialists and bankers, who were either very wealthy or lived an upper-middle-class life. The blue-collar class also expanded exponentially; after all, industries could only grow and prosper as a result of the working class. The poorer classes mostly consisted of new immigrants, who arrived in droves.

While there were a number of rising industrialists and bankers, there was a handful who were considered the most prominent and powerful. They left behind an enduring legacy.

John D. Rockefeller

John D. Rockefeller, a Republican, championed many social reforms and was considered to be a very progressive and liberal man. He became wealthy by dominating the oil industry, which also had a profound impact on the Industrial Revolution.

He founded the company Standard Oil and controlled nearly 90 percent of the oil refineries all over America.

John D. Rockefeller.
https://commons.wikimedia.org/wiki/File:Portrait_of_J._D._Rockefeller.jpg

Rockefeller's refineries turned oil into kerosene, the product used by Americans in their homes. Some people admired him greatly, while others felt he was unethical and immoral.

Rockefeller was often criticized by journalists, reformers, and other people for the way he made his money. He was accused of being greedy and of building his empire by crushing the competition through secret dealings and threats. He also took advantage of other people's failures to enrich himself.

Most businessmen likely engaged in similar tactics to build their wealth, so the criticisms may not be entirely fair. What we do know of Rockefeller is that he treated his workers fairly and well. He praised where praise was due, ensured his workers felt respected, and was even known to occasionally work alongside them.

Whatever one's opinion, there is no doubt that he did a lot for society. He retired in 1896 and spent the rest of his life doing philanthropy. He championed public sanitation and helped with the fight against diseases like yellow fever and malaria. Rockefeller also funded schools and organizations to help the next generation move forward.

His legacy endures to this day, as the Rockefeller Foundation continues to champion causes that affect society.

Andrew Carnegie

Known and revered as one of the most successful businessmen in American history, Andrew Carnegie came from very humble beginnings and went on to become one of the richest men in America. His fortune was built through the steel industry.

Carnegie co-founded a steel company in the early 1870s and spent decades building it into a steel empire. He was innovative and worked hard to bring down the cost of steel and make it more affordable. He purchased iron mines and railroad companies, which allowed him to reduce his own costs, which, in turn, meant he could sell his steel at a reduced cost.

Andrew Carnegie also adopted a new invention that allowed steel to be made from iron in a more efficient manner. His steel mills were incredibly modern and served as a model to be emulated by other companies in the industry.

Thanks to his fight to lower prices, America was able to start building skyscrapers at a reasonable cost. The United States' first skyscraper, the Home Insurance Company Building, began construction in Chicago in 1884 using steel girders.

Carnegie's treatment of his workers was anything but generous and has generated a lot of controversy over the years. His workers worked twelve-hour days, seven days a week. They had no holidays or days off besides the Fourth of July. The working conditions were harsh and dangerous, and the workers' wages were barely enough to get by. Carnegie cut those meager wages further to keep a higher profit.

Work-related deaths were not uncommon. In 1880, an explosion occurred in one of his factories that resulted in several workers dying. Carnegie was more concerned with the material losses incurred than the lives lost, which cast him in a villainous light.

Carnegie's wealth was built on the backs of the mill workers, yet he seemed to care very little about them. It's hard to understand why he would treat his workers in such a way when he had been born and raised in a very humble and hard environment.

However, he was known for being generous and became a great philanthropist in his later years. He donated the bulk of his wealth to charitable causes. Carnegie was a great champion of education and helped to establish schools, colleges, and other nonprofit organizations like public libraries, museums, and even a music hall.

Andrew Carnegie's s contributions to American society cannot be denied, but neither can his treatment of the men and women who built him his empire.

J. P. Morgan

John Pierpont Morgan was one of the most powerful bankers in the Progressive Era. He had a particular talent for bringing stability to a business and making it profitable. He became an extremely powerful railroad magnate by reorganizing and merging several railroad companies and buying stock in those companies.

In 1898, he did something similar with steel and provided financing for the creation of the Federal Steel Company. Morgan later merged several steel companies and created the United States Steel Corporation. Through a number of strategic and bold moves, he amassed a fortune.

When the United States was facing economic crises, it had no way of handling them because the country did not have a central bank. Morgan stepped in to loan over $60 million to the government, helping to rescue the country's gold standard. Aside from helping the federal government with the economy, Morgan also helped Roosevelt bring an end to the Coal Strike of 1902.

Morgan would go on to become the head of the banking firm known as J. P. Morgan & Co. Today, the bank is one of the largest financial institutions in the world.

Like Rockefeller and Carnegie, he contributed a lot to society and donated millions of dollars to educational institutions, museums, and other public institutions.

There are arguments to be made about how much good the rich industrialists and bankers brought to society. They typically used dubious means to acquire their wealth and used their money and influence to impact politics and the government. But it cannot be denied that their philanthropical work helped shape society as we know it today.

PART FIVE:
WWI, Great Depression, and WWII (1914–1945)

Thanks in large part to the rapid industrial growth, a surge in global exports, waves of immigration, and a booming economy, the United States was slowly but surely gaining a global reputation as a rising and influential power. But America's handling of the First and Second World Wars would cement its position as a worldwide superpower.

Chapter 18: World War I and the Roaring '20s

US and WWI

For decades, the United States had steadfastly maintained a position of isolationism when it came to world events. It was more concerned with its own expansion and growth.

So, when Austrian Archduke Franz Ferdinand was assassinated by the Black Hand, a Serbian nationalist group, on June 28th, 1914, it wasn't seen as a monumental event in the United States, or at least an event worth getting involved with.

Of course, nobody could have predicted that the assassination would set off a chain of events, ultimately leading to a global conflict between the Allies (France, Russia, Great Britain, Serbia, and eventually the United States) and the Central Powers (Germany, the Ottoman Empire, and Austria-Hungary).

President Woodrow Wilson and WWI

When the war broke out, the United States had no interest and no stakes in the conflict. President Woodrow Wilson openly declared that America would remain neutral. The majority of the American public supported this stance, especially since there were many immigrants in the country whose nations were at war with each other in Europe. Wilson felt it was a delicate issue all around and best to be avoided.

As a neutral country, the US provided raw materials, food, and ammunition to both sides. Banks also provided loans to the countries at war; however, most of these resources and loans went to the Allied countries.

Public sentiment began to shift in May 1915 after the *Lusitania*, a British ship, was sunk by a German U-boat. Approximately 1,200 people died, 128 of them Americans. The war had finally hit close to home, and the diplomatic relationship between the US and Germany became tense.

President Wilson provided a strict warning to Germany but still wanted to stay neutral. Many Americans disagreed with him. Germany torpedoed a French ship in March 1916, and when the US threatened to cut diplomatic ties, Germany promised not to sink any more merchant or passenger ships.

In November 1916, Wilson won a second term as president. By this time, some Americans headed to Europe to help the war effort.

By the end of January 1917, Germany announced that it would resume its submarine warfare. America finally cut off diplomatic ties with the country, and over the next two months, several American merchant ships were attacked and sunk by German U-boats.

The final straw for the American government was the Zimmerman telegram. The telegram outlined an alliance between Germany and Mexico, with Germany pledging to help Mexico regain territories it had lost to America in exchange for support with the war. When the telegram became public knowledge, Americans were beyond outraged. On April 2nd, 1917, President Wilson officially declared war on Germany and entered **WWI**. Their entry provided a much-needed boost for the war-weary British and French. Through the course of the war, nearly 120,000 American soldiers died.

Wilson and the League of Nations

Once the US entered the war, it was determined to win the conflict. Wilson was horrified by the destruction and brutality of the war and wanted to ensure that such a thing would never occur again. Wilson unveiled his Fourteen Points in early 1918, which were a set of guidelines that he believed would deter another war.

With the Fourteen Points, Wilson outlined his vision of establishing an international organization whose task would be to resolve global disputes before they could get out of hand. He also believed that nations should be open and transparent and that all countries had the right to self-determination.

When the war ended, Allied leaders met in Paris to hash out the terms of peace. Wilson worked hard to make the treaty as fair as he could, given the European countries' intense anger toward Germany. The terms of the treaty put the blame of the entire war on Germany, leaving the country humiliated and in financial ruin. Germany was also forced to demilitarize its forces. The Treaty of Versailles, which ended one world war, would ironically go on to become one of the causes of another world war.

The Paris Peace Conference of 1919 resulted in the Treaty of Versailles, which included a pledge to create the League of Nations. The League of Nations was based largely on Wilson's Fourteen Points and was created to make sure that something like WWI never happened again. The League of Nations had four main goals:

1. To settle disputes and conflicts between countries through peaceful means before they could escalate into anything more serious
2. Improve global welfare
3. Promote collective security
4. Disarmament

Despite Wilson's best efforts to get the United States involved in the League of Nations, Congress was unwilling to consider it. For Congress, American involvement in WWI was a one-time thing. Once it was over, they wanted to go back to their isolationist stance. Congress especially took issue with Article X of the League, which stated that all members of the League had to defend another member country if it faced aggression or in the event of an attack. This was something Congress was not willing to commit to, as they felt the term violated American sovereignty. Due to this opposition, the Treaty of Versailles was not ratified by the Senate, and the US never became part of the League of Nations.

The League was in existence until 1946. Although it failed to prevent WWII, it did negotiate some conflicts peacefully, for instance, Turkey's and Iraq's dispute over Mosul in 1926. Shortly before it was dissolved, the United Nations was created. The UN was based on the same premise and principles as the League of Nations but did not have its weaknesses. The UN also had a lot more support from other countries than the League of Nations did.

By this point, the US felt as if it had a leadership role to play in international politics, so the country was involved with the organization from the very start.

Prohibition

There was a significant revival of religion in the United States in the early 19th century. Some movements called for the abolishment of slavery while also calling for temperance.

In 1838, the state of Massachusetts passed a temperance law. The law only lasted for two years, but it set the wheels in motion for other states to follow suit, like Maine, which passed a stricter law regarding alcohol in 1846.

By the time the Civil War started, many other states had similar laws in place, and temperance societies had become the norm in American society. Women were especially against the consumption of alcohol because they saw the damage it could wreak. Even factory owners were on board with prohibition because they had fewer accidents, and their workers were more efficient and productive.

By 1917, World War I was well under way. America had just joined the Allies when President Woodrow Wilson enacted a wartime prohibition legislation so that grain could be saved for food. Around this time, Congress also submitted the Eighteenth Amendment for ratification.

The amendment was ratified in 1919 and went into effect in 1920. By this time, thirty-three states already had their own prohibition laws. Under the amendment, the sale, transportation, and manufacture of alcoholic beverages became illegal, ushering in the era of Prohibition.

In 1919, Congress put out the National Prohibition Act (commonly referred to as the Volstead Act). This act provided the government with guidelines on how to enforce the legislation. However, even with new legislation and an act in place, it was nearly impossible to enforce Prohibition or eradicate alcohol.

Bootlegging (making, selling, and smuggling alcohol illegally) inevitably led to the rise of organized crime and other illegal operations. It became a dangerous but very lucrative profession. Well-known gangster Al Capone used to make approximately $60 million every year through bootlegging.

This, in turn, led to an increase in gang violence. Businesses, such as restaurants that could no longer sell alcohol, suffered, and many went out of business. Other people died or put their health at risk by drinking homemade liquor like moonshine, which was often tainted. Revenues for the government and the states tumbled.

Prohibition became nearly impossible to control. By the time the 1920s were coming to an end, so was the public's support for Prohibition. By the time the Great Depression hit, the idea of legalizing alcohol again and making money from it was too tempting to resist. When Franklin Delano Roosevelt ran for the presidency in 1932, he promised to repeal the law if elected.

FDR easily beat out Herbert Hoover, and as promised, in February 1933, the Twenty-first Amendment was officially put forward to repeal the Eighteenth Amendment. By December of that year, thirty-six states voted in favor, and it was ratified. Some states continued to hold on to Prohibition. By 1966, none of the states enforced Prohibition anymore.

The Roaring '20s

After the war and the 1918 influenza pandemic, which killed more people than the war did (between fifty and one hundred million), came to an end, Americans entered a new uproarious period of dramatic social and economic changes filled with unrestrained joy and mirth.

Technological progress, industrialization, and the mass production of goods led to the rise of consumerism. As Americans prospered, they began moving away from farms to settle in cities. Employment was at a high, credit was available for cheap, America's GDP more than doubled, and the country saw rapid economic growth. The years of hardship and wartime devastation felt like a story of the past.

All of this led to the emergence of the Roaring '20s or the Jazz Age, a period characterized by growth and change. It would also be the first decade in American history that would be given a nickname.

Before WWI, American culture was still very much following the traditions of the 19th century. But post-WWI, the people were ready to usher in a new era. And it would be a modern, liberating era with dance halls, cinemas, flappers, jazz music, and speakeasies.

Women emerged from their traditional roles to embrace independence and make themselves heard. Flappers courted a lot of controversy with their short bob hairstyle, makeup, scandalous clothes, and a free-spirited lifestyle of smoking and dancing to jazz bands.

An example of a flapper.
https://commons.wikimedia.org/wiki/File:Violet_Romer_in_flapper_dress,_LC-DIG-ggbain-12393_crop.jpg

Fueled by the victory of the Nineteenth Amendment, an ever-increasing number of women began to join the workforce and push for personal freedom.

The Roaring '20s was also a time of artistic expression, new inventions, and industrial growth. The hours for blue-collar workers fell to forty-four hours per week while salaries were increased. Americans suddenly had more money and more time for fun and enjoyable activities like going to the cinema (films had just started to come out), attending dance halls, and watching Babe Ruth play baseball.

Clever marketing linked happiness and success to material goods. Americans bought cars, radios, and other goods, which changed the way they lived and enjoyed life. Technological advancements meant more people had access to electricity, which meant commercial goods like fridges and vacuum cleaners became household necessities for middle-class families, something that was unimaginable at the start of the 1900s.

And then, just as suddenly as it began, the Jazz Age came to a halt as the stock market crashed in October 1929. Prior to the crash, people had invested millions of dollars in the stock market during a period of speculation. When the market crashed, investors lost a combined total of $26 billion and made paupers out of people overnight.

The economic boom and the Roaring '20s were suddenly over, ushering in the period called the Great Depression.

Chapter 19: The Great Depression and the New Deal

Great Depression (1929-1939)

The Great Depression is typically associated with the collapse of the stock market, and while it was definitely a factor, it wasn't the only reason for the dramatic shift in the country's economy.

To this day, the Great Depression remains one of the worst economic downturns to ever be faced by America and the world at large. Millions of Americans were affected by it. Fortunes disappeared, and people lost their homes and could not afford to eat. Thousands of people lived in shanty towns called Hoovervilles just to have a roof over their heads. The term referenced President Herbert Hoover, who promised that wealth and good times were just around the corner.

For Americans who were receiving very little government assistance or support, comments like this were laughable. Unemployment rose to 25.6 percent at one point, meaning one in four Americans had no source of income and no hope for it either.

When historians look back today on why there was such a change between the 1920s and the 1930s, they look at a few factors that, individually, would have been surmountable but became totally disastrous when combined.

1. The global economy was vulnerable due to high consumer demand and a lack of financial cooperation between nations internationally.
2. The rise of wealth during the Jazz Age made people believe that one could get rich overnight through investments and stocks. People easily fell victim to cons or bad investments. The number of people buying stocks increased dramatically, making prices soar. For a time, this made a lot of people very wealthy, but on Black Thursday—the day the stock market crashed—the bubble finally burst. Within a month, the Dow's value halved, and it kept going down.
3. In the early 1920s, money was plentiful, and interest rates were down, which led to people taking out loans and credit. By the end of the '20s, the Federal Board was concerned about speculation and suddenly raised interest rates, making it harder for people to pay things back or buy new things.
4. When the stock market crashed, investors began to exchange cash for gold, so interest rates were hiked up again as a way of protecting the dollar. But this meant that businesses could no longer afford to take out loans to stay afloat and had to shut down.
5. The Smoot-Hawley Act was a policy that raised US tariffs by approximately 16 percent. When Congress first debated the act in 1929, the economy was still in good shape. But after it was signed in 1930, things started to go badly. Other countries began to add tariffs on goods exported from the US because of the act.

A combination of these factors created a perfect storm for the economy to tumble and usher in a decade of hardship and deprivation. A period of drought also added to the hardships.

The Dust Bowl

A period of intense dust storms damaged and ruined crops in the prairie lands of North America in the 1930s. This terrible time in US history was called the Dust Bowl. Clouds of dust blew continuously for days, falling like snow. The dust even fell through the cracks of people's homes. The storms led to people and livestock dying and crops failing. Entire regions were left decimated and ruined. The dust also impacted people's health, as some people developed chest pains and other health problems.

The dust storms were caused by a combination of poor farming techniques, extremely hot weather, prolonged drought, and severe winds. These factors created the perfect storm for dust bowls to sweep through the states of Texas, Colorado, Kansas, New Mexico, Oklahoma, and Nebraska.

The continuous dust storms, also known as "black blizzards," forced thousands of people to leave their homes and become migrants as they looked for work and a better quality of life. Around two and a half million people left the dust bowl states; it was the largest migration of people in the country.

To help the people, President Franklin Delano Roosevelt provided emergency relief to affected people. Farmers were resettled on different lands that were more productive, and aid was provided to migrant farm workers.

Roosevelt also wanted to solve the environmental problems so that this wouldn't happen again. The government planted over 200 million trees to prevent the soil from blowing over the Great Plains. The trees also helped with the wind. Within five years, the benefits could be seen. By 1938, the efforts had reduced the blowing soil by 65 percent.

For the most part, the Dust Bowl came to an end in 1939 when rain returned to many of the dry areas.

New Deal Programs

During the 1932 presidential election, Franklin D. Roosevelt (FDR for short) defeated Hoover and won the presidency in a landslide. He took office while America was facing its greatest economic crisis in history.

FDR knew he had to do something to solve the crisis. During his inauguration speech on March 4th, 1933, he promised as much to the people. Two days after his speech, FDR shut down all the banks across America for a period of four days so people would stop taking out money from banks that were already unstable. About nine thousand banks had already closed during the Great Depression.

Through Roosevelt's Emergency Banking Act, which was passed on March 9th, the banks that were insolvent were shut down permanently, while the rest were reorganized. Americans were urged to put their money back into the banks, and surprisingly, people began to do so.

This was FDR's first step toward his goal of ending the Great Depression. He swiftly got to work to solve the problems the public was facing and came up with the New Deal. The New Deal was a series of financial reforms, public projects, and other programs and regulations that were established to stabilize the economy and bring financial relief to struggling Americans.

FDR also requested that Congress end Prohibition, which it did by ratifying the Twenty-first Amendment.

The Tennessee Valley Authority Act was signed into law several months later in May. Under this law, the government was allowed to build dams down the Tennessee River to control issues with flooding. Another bill was passed by Congress that paid some farmers not to plant anything on their fields to increase the prices of agricultural products and to end the surpluses.

Workers were given the right to create and be part of unions through the National Industrial Recovery Act, which also led to the creation of the Public Works Administration. This act allowed workers to collectively ask for better wages and working conditions.

In addition to these acts and legislations, FDR passed a dozen other laws, including a banking bill and a Home Owners' Loan Act. All of this was accomplished in his first one hundred days as president!

Second New Deal

Despite FDR's aggressive approach to tackling the Great Depression, the financial crisis continued. Unemployment was still at a high, the economy was still struggling, and most Americans continued to be filled with desperation and anger.

So, FDR launched a second round of federal programs in 1935, which is often referred to as the Second New Deal. One of the first programs to be launched was the Works Progress Administration (WPA). Under this program, unemployed people were given jobs in the public sector to build things like schools, parks, and bridges.

The program also created jobs for people in the arts by hiring writers and artists.

The National Labor Relations Board was created in July 1935 to maintain the integrity of union elections and to ensure that employers did not treat their workers poorly or unfairly. The Social Security Act, which was drafted in the same year, provided unemployment insurance. The government also pledged that children and disabled people would be cared for.

While the New Deal helped resolve some issues, it still faced many political setbacks, especially from the conservatives on the Supreme Court, who pulled back initiatives like the National Recovery Administration, which sought to establish fair workplace practices.

But FDR was not deterred. He refused to allow the Supreme Court to keep changing his programs, so in 1937, he announced that more liberal justices would be added to the Supreme Court so that there could be a better balance. When the justices discovered this, they started to vote in favor of FDR's projects. All the while, the Great Depression dragged on.

Economy and Culture

In 1937, the economy was back in a recession, and Roosevelt was having difficulty pushing forward new programs or policies. Two years later, the New Deal began to fizzle and eventually came to an end. World War II would ultimately bring the US economy back on top.

But the work FDR did on the New Deal programs between 1933 and 1941 greatly improved the lives of people who were struggling during the Depression. It gave them hope in a particularly difficult time. It also changed the political and social landscape of American society by creating the conditions for the emergence of a new political coalition, which suddenly included a more diverse group of Americans, including African Americans and working-class Americans. They were linked together in their common desire to see programs like Social Security succeed.

There was also a huge cultural shift, as more women began working outside the home. Roosevelt facilitated this by increasing the number of administrative and secretarial jobs in the government.

FDR's programs created the foundation for present-day America. Many of the things Americans take for granted today, like welfare and unemployment insurance, stem from the New Deal.

Chapter 20: WWII: America Becomes a Superpower

World War II

After more than a decade of suffering, the Great Depression came to an end when Japan bombed Pearl Harbor.

However, that wasn't the start of the war. When Adolf Hitler broke the terms of the Munich Agreement and invaded Czechoslovakia, the United States stayed out of it, even as it became apparent that war was inevitable. And when war broke out when Hitler invaded Poland in 1939, the US government fell back on its isolationist foreign policy and remained neutral for the first two years of the war.

The Neutrality Act passed by Congress in 1935 specifically prohibited the US from exporting any arms, money, supplies, or ammunition to any countries that were at war. After the Spanish Civil War of 1936-1939, the act was amended to be even more stringent and included greater restrictions.

All of this made it very difficult for FDR to get involved in the war, even though he firmly believed the country should. He had the foresight to see what Hitler's invasion meant for the world, and he knew America had a role to play in stopping him.

So, he found creative ways to bend the rules. For example, pilots flew WWI-era aircraft from the US and left them just a few feet away from the Canadian border. The Canadians took it from there and sent them to Allied forces in Europe.

But when Hitler got bolder and invaded Poland, triggering the start of WWII, it became more difficult to remain neutral and do nothing. Congress was eventually persuaded to amend the act to implement a "cash and carry" policy. Under this, Allied powers fighting Germany could purchase supplies made in America using "cash" and then "carry: it back to Europe on their own ships or planes.

Lend-Lease Policy

This worked well until Germany invaded and then occupied France, leaving Great Britain to battle it out alone against Hitler in western Europe. Newly elected British Prime Minister Winston Churchill reached out to FDR to tell him Britain was running out of money and would soon be unable to pay for supplies.

FDR had won his reelection for his third term as president with the promise to keep America out of the war, but he still wanted to help, so he convinced Americans and Congress that providing help to the Allies was in their best interest.

By the end of 1940, a new policy was introduced, allowing America to lend supplies to Britain for the war. Under this policy, payments wouldn't need to be made in cash and could be in a form acceptable to Roosevelt. The payments would also be deferred. FDR assured the American people that they had a critical role to play as the "great arsenal of democracy."[6]

After months of debate, Congress passed the Lend-Lease Act in March 1941, and FDR began to place orders for supplies, tanks, ships, weapons, and food to send to Great Britain. Within the year, the Lend-Lease program was expanded to include allies like Russia, and it kept being extended. In total, over the course of the war, over thirty countries around the world received $50 billion of aid from the US through the program (equivalent to $690 billion today).

---

[6] "Lend-Lease Act." https://www.history.com/topics/world-war-ii/lend-lease-act-1.

America Joins the War

After staying neutral, the United States was finally forced to join the war when Japan bombed Pearl Harbor in Hawaii on December 7th, 1941. Over 2,400 American troops and nearly seventy civilians died in the attack. Nineteen ships, including eight battleships, were destroyed. Americans were incensed at the carnage.

Within a day, Congress declared war on Japan, prompting the Axis powers to declare war on the US. This would become a turning point for the war, which, so far, seemed to be going better for Hitler and his Axis allies than for the Allied powers.

At home, the war was changing the way society functioned. Women were starting to enter the workforce in droves and enjoyed a newfound sense of purpose and freedom. Concerts, fundraising activities, and victory gardens all created a feeling of patriotism amongst Americans and added to the feeling of unity and standing up for what was right.

The war also created some ugliness at home, as the government created internment camps to house Japanese Americans. Since the Allies were fighting against Japan, there was a natural distrust toward Japan and its people. This spilled over into distrust, dislike, and even hatred of the Japanese people in America, who had previously been neighbors, friends, and co-workers. Through Executive Order 9066, Japanese people were rounded up and sent to camps that were scattered throughout the US.

They would remain incarcerated, living in poor conditions for the duration of the war. Almost two thousand died. Families were displaced and torn apart forever. When the Japanese were eventually released and allowed to return to their lives, they found everything they had worked for was gone. The effects of their incarceration would last for generations.

Meanwhile, American troops took part in dozens of battles and conflicts on numerous fronts, although the US played more of a leadership role in the Pacific theater. We have selected a handful of the most significant battles fought by the US.

Battle of the Coral Sea (May 4th-May 8th, 1942)

The Battle of the Coral Sea was significant because it was the first time that a major Japanese operation had been stopped.

Japanese forces managed to successfully occupy the island of Tulagi, but American troops, who had been expecting the invasion, tried to intercept the Japanese troops. For four days, the two air powers engaged in an intense battle, which resulted in the destruction of sixty-six warplanes on the American side and seventy on the Japanese side.

This battle was interesting because neither country's carriers fired shots at each other. Instead, as the planes took off from the carriers, they battled against each other. This battle and style of warfare was a foreshadowing of how the battles on the Pacific front would play out.

The battle was a tactical victory for Japan, which succeeded in occupying all of the Solomon Islands and destroyed several key Allied ships, including the fleet carrier *Lexington*. However, it came at a great cost since Japan couldn't continue with its planned invasions of Port Moresby and other targets in the South Pacific, which had been its primary objectives.

When Japan met the US again at the Battle of Midway, it was in a much weaker position.

Battle of Midway (June 3rd-June 6th, 1942)

While Hitler's target was Europe, Japan had its sights set firmly on dominating the Pacific. Its first hurdle in its plan was the setback faced at the Battle of the Coral Sea, which forced it to turn away from its other targets.

However, the commander of the Imperial Japanese Navy, Admiral Isoroku Yamamoto, was convinced they could defeat the Americans by replicating another attack similar to Pearl Harbor. He planned to launch another surprise attack against the American troops on Midway Island, which was being used as a naval base for the Allies. Ideally located between the two countries, it was the perfect target for Japan.

Yamamoto meticulously planned a three-pronged attack. There would be an air attack, followed by a naval invasion. Then, once American reinforcements arrived, they would engage in battle. The problem with the plan was that cryptanalysts in the US Navy had been decoding Japan's communication codes since 1942 and knew about Yamamoto's plans. They figured out that Midway was the target.

On June 3rd, an American reconnaissance plane spied what it believed was the majority of the Japanese fleet. Later that afternoon, American bombers struck at the target but were unsuccessful.

A scene from the Battle of Midway.
https://commons.wikimedia.org/wiki/File:SBD-3_Dauntless_bombers_of_VS-8_over_the_burning_Japanese_cruiser_Mikuma_on_6_June_1942.jpg

A second attack from the US took place the following morning, which was again unsuccessful. Japan then sent over one hundred warplanes to Midway and significantly damaged the base. American torpedo bombers carried on the *Hornet* and *Enterprise* began an attack on Japan's ships, but they were all shot down.

A second wave of US bombers arrived an hour later and set fire to the Japanese carriers. Additional US dive bombers continued attacking. By this point, Yamamoto knew that the battle had been lost. He retreated on June 6th, bringing the Battle of Midway to an end.

It was a decisive and critical victory for the Americans, as it put a stop to Japan's plans to expand its empire in the Pacific. The battle started to turn the tide of the war in favor of the Allies.

D-Day (June 6th, 1944)

One of the most significant battles and victories for the Allied powers during the war was the Battle of Normandy, commonly referred to as D-Day and codenamed Operation Overlord. The goal was to take back France from German occupation.

When the US joined the war, the main strategy was "Germany first," meaning the priority was to defeat Germany and Hitler. But the British wanted to focus on campaigns in Italy and North Africa before going after Hitler. The US didn't agree with that approach, but nonetheless, the early waves of American troops were sent to support the British in their other campaigns away from Germany. Operation Overlord was delayed until 1944.

Normandy was chosen as the location of the invasion because it was less defended and not the obvious choice. Allied powers set up decoys to trick the Nazis about the location of the invasion. Hitler fell for the trick and scattered his resources.

Prior to the Allied landings, the beaches were bombed heavily to clear the area. Bridges and roads were destroyed so Germany couldn't easily get reinforcements or leave. After the bombings, paratroopers were dropped behind the beaches to secure the ground in preparation for the land invasion. The beaches were codenamed Utah, Gold, Omaha, Sword, and Juno.

Despite careful planning, things started off rocky. The weather delayed the invasion. Some of the bombers missed key targets that had to be taken out, and many paratroopers landed in the wrong place, often ending up in enemy hands. Some tanks and vital equipment sank before making it to shore.

An iconic image of the landing at Omaha Beach.

https://en.wikipedia.org/wiki/File:Into_the_Jaws_of_Death_23-0455M_edit.jpg

The forces landing from the sea began the invasion on June 6th, 1944, at 6:30 a.m. Gold, Juno, Utah, and Sword were easily captured. However, Omaha faced heavy resistance from German troops, and the Americans suffered more than two thousand casualties.

Through the course of the day, the Allied powers managed to successfully storm the beaches. Within a week, the beaches were completely secured. As more troops and equipment arrived in Normandy, Allied forces were able to push back German troops in France, although the fighting was bloody and intense.

In August, Allied troops arrived at the Seine River, and France was soon liberated. With German troops pushed out of northwestern France and Paris secured, the Battle of Normandy was over.

End of the War

The victory at Normandy turned the tide of the war against Germany. With France no longer under his control, Hitler was unable to build his Western Front as he had planned and thus had no protection against the Soviets when they began to advance.

After France, the Allied powers turned toward Germany and eventually made Hitler fight the war on two fronts.

The Battle of Berlin (April 16th–May 2nd, 1945)

When Russia and the Allies joined forces, they had one common goal: to get rid of Hitler. After Italy's surrender to the Allies on September 8th, 1943, and the liberation of France, it was clear that Germany was losing ground.

By 1945, the Allies were fully focused on defeating Germany. Daytime raids on Berlin by the US air forces became a regular occurrence. Starting in March 1945, British RAF (Royal Air Force) Mosquitos dropped bombs on the city every night for more than a month.

The bombings stopped when Soviet troops marched into Berlin on April 16th, officially starting the Battle of Berlin. Within days, the Soviets, who vastly outnumbered the Germans, had surrounded the city. The fighting between the two sides became violent and fierce.

By the end of the month, the Soviets were close to the center of the city. It was clear to everyone, Hitler included, that defeat was imminent. Knowing the war was lost, Hitler decided to commit suicide on April 30th, 1945.

On May 2nd, the city garrison surrendered, but the fighting only fully stopped on May 8th. Berlin stayed under Russian occupation until Western Allied troops arrived in Berlin two months later and took charge of the occupation.

Liberation of Dachau – April 1945

Ending the war in Europe and getting rid of Hitler and the Nazis also meant the end of the Holocaust and the liberation of the concentration camps.

Dachau was the first concentration camp the Nazis built. Within weeks of Hitler becoming

chancellor, the plans for Dachau were well underway. Originally intended to house political prisoners, the camp would go on to play a crucial role in the Holocaust.

In the camp's first year of existence, around five thousand people, mainly German communists and political opponents, were imprisoned at the camp. Over the next few years, the number of prisoners grew substantially to include Roma people, criminals, gay people, and anyone else that Hitler or the Nazis deemed "undesirable." The prisoners were put to work to construct new additions to the camp.

Starting in 1938, the majority of the prisoners became Jews. When the Holocaust started in earnest, the other concentration camps were closely modeled on Dachau, which became a training center for Hitler's concentration camp guards. Medical experiments using humans also began in Dachau.

Once the Allied forces began to win the war and started to advance into Germany, prisoners from other concentration camps were transferred to Dachau. The march of the mostly Jewish prisoners is often referred to as the "death march." By late April 1945, American troops were already in Germany, and on April 29th, three US Army divisions arrived at Dachau. American soldiers witnessed the horrors of the Holocaust.

A small skirmish with the SS guards followed before the camp was officially liberated, and the Prisoners were freed. The same day, another group of American troops, the 42nd Rainbow Division, liberated a subcamp of Dachau.

Battle of Okinawa – April 1st–June 22nd, 1945

One of the bloodiest battles of the Second World War was also its last major battle. While Allied troops were advancing into Germany, bringing the war in Europe to an end, the US Navy, the Marine Corps, and the US Army, along with other Allied contingents, were busy pushing the Japanese off the island of Okinawa in the Pacific.

The war in the Pacific theater raged on with one battle after another. American troops had destroyed Japan in the Battle of Iwo Jima, and now they turned to Okinawa. Securing the bases on the island was the final hurdle before they could reach Japan. Okinawa was the perfect place for the Japanese to mount a final defense.

On April 1st, 1945, American troops bombarded the beaches to allow for troop landings, similar to what was done for D-Day. Morale was low, and the Allies expected a strong Japanese resistance. Instead, waves of tanks, supplies, and troops were able to come ashore with virtually no opposition.

Within hours, American soldiers secured the Kadena and Yontan airfields. Unbeknownst to them, they were falling perfectly into the trap set out by Lieutenant General Mitsuru Ushijima, the man leading Japan's 32nd Army. The 130,000 men had been told not to fire on the Americans; instead, they were told to watch as they waited in defensive positions.

As the Americans came farther inland, the battle started in earnest. The fighting was fierce and bloody, and both sides lost a staggering number of people. The Japanese engaged in kamikaze warfare (suicide attacks). The Americans succeeded in pushing the Japanese back toward the southern coast of the island.

On April 7th, a Japanese battleship, *Yamato*, prepared to launch an attack on the US troops, but it was spotted by the Allied powers. The ship was bombed and sunk. A crucial battle on Hacksaw Ridge took place on April 26th. By this point, the soldiers on both sides were engaging in vicious, hand-to-hand combat. The fighting was intense and brutal. Ten days later, on May 6th, the Americans were able to successfully take Hacksaw Ridge. Instead of surrendering, many Japanese soldiers chose to kill themselves, including General Ushijima and his chief of staff.

By June 22nd, most of the Japanese resistance operations had been taken down. The Americans lost 12,520 men, and over 36,000 soldiers were wounded. The Japanese lost around 110,000 soldiers, and it is believed that nearly as many Okinawa citizens died, some of whom committed suicide after Japanese soldiers lied to them about what lay in store if the Americans won the battle.

The Nuclear Era
The Manhattan Project

Despite Germany's surrender, the war was technically not over. Japan was still fighting, and it refused to surrender. With Germany under control, the Allied powers, especially US President Harry Truman, who took over after FDR died on April 12th, 1945, were determined to get Japan to surrender and bring the war to a quick and definite end. Truman's plan to bring the war to a swift end worked, but it would have far-reaching repercussions and consequences for decades to follow.

In 1938, German physicists in Berlin discovered nuclear fission, which opened the door to exploring the creation of nuclear weapons. And that's exactly what happened.

While the war was going on, other countries worried that Germany would develop nuclear weapons to use during the war. Several nations began to try and develop nuclear weapons themselves, including the United States. The project to develop the atomic bomb was officially authorized by FDR on December 28th, 1942, and given the codename the Manhattan Project.

A number of scientists and officials, led by Robert Oppenheimer, began working on the top-secret project in Los Alamos, New Mexico. At one point, 130,000 people were part of the project. Two and a half years after the project began, three atomic bombs were developed by scientists. One of the bombs was tested in a desert in New Mexico on July 16th, 1945. The project was deemed a great success.

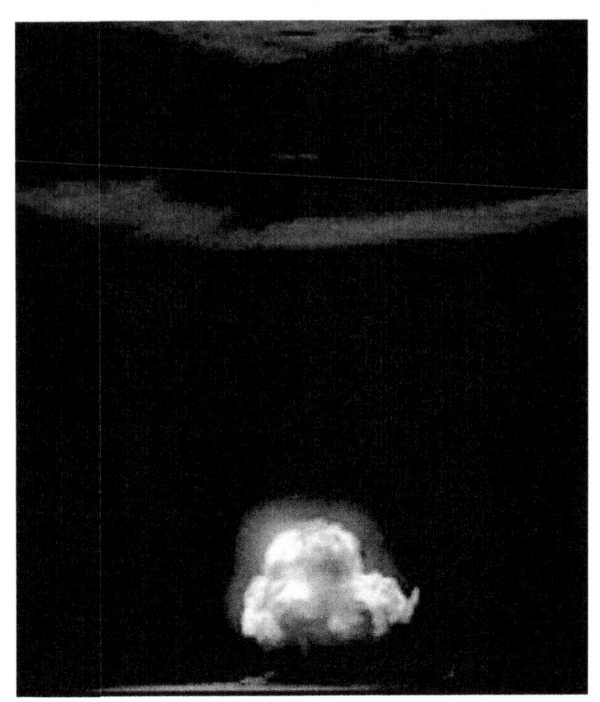

The Trinity Test, the first nuclear test explosion.
https://commons.wikimedia.org/wiki/File:Trinity_shot_color.jpg

The United States had managed to build the first atomic bomb.

Hiroshima and Nagasaki

By the time the bomb was tested, the war in Europe was already over. Germany had surrendered, the fighting had stopped, and peace negotiations were being started.

However, the fighting between Japan and the Allies, namely the United States, continued. Toward the end of July, President Harry Truman announced the Potsdam Declaration, which stated that if Japan refused to surrender, the US would take harsh and destructive action. Japan refused.

After much back and forth, President Truman then made the difficult decision to drop an atomic bomb on the country. The *Enola Gay*, a bomber plane, carried the first bomb, dropping it on Hiroshima on August 6th, 1945, destroying large parts of the city. Between 70,000 and 135,000 people died that same year, while tens of thousands died later from radiation or other bomb-related causes.

Japan still refused to surrender. Perhaps the government believed the US wouldn't use another bomb on them after seeing the devastation or that the US would have used all its bombs at once to get rid of Japan for good.

Whatever the reasoning, three days later, on August 9th, a second bomb was dropped on Nagasaki, leading to between sixty thousand and eighty thousand deaths that same year (it is hard to know exactly how many died instantly, which makes sense due to the lack of manpower to tally such high counts and sift through the wreckage in a reasonable amount of time).

Hiroshima after the bombing.
https://commons.wikimedia.org/wiki/File:Hiroshima_aftermath.jpg

Japanese Emperor Hirohito surrendered six days later. Thus, August 15th became known as VJ Day or "Victory over Japan Day." Some historians believe that the Soviet Union's invasion of Japan would have been enough to make the Japanese surrender. Truman's reasoning behind using the atomic bombs was to save his men, as the Japanese threatened to fight to the very end. However, innocent people were killed. As you can likely tell, the atomic bombings remain a controversial topic to this day.

A formal surrender from Japan took place on September 2nd in Tokyo Bay on the USS *Missouri*. After six long and devastating years, the global conflict was over.

However, the effects of the bombing would last for decades, as people died of leukemia and cancer and suffered from the horrible side effects of nuclear radiation. It is estimated that hundreds of thousands of people died in the two cities because of post-radiation effects, but the actual number may never be known.

Occupation of Japan

When Japan surrendered to the Allies on September 2nd, 1945, it officially ended the Second World War. Between 1945 and 1952, Japan was occupied by the Allied powers. The occupation was mostly overseen by the American forces, who were led by General Douglas MacArthur.

The US had two very specific goals for the occupation. It wanted to eliminate Japan as a possible threat in the future by demilitarizing the country, and it also wanted Japan to become a democratic nation, one closely allied with the Western world.

During the period of occupation, the American government invested $2.2 billion (around $18 billion today) in Japan's reconstruction and helped stabilize the country. Under MacArthur, a new constitution was created, which replaced the Meiji Constitution that had been written in 1889. Power was put in the hands of elected officials and not the emperor, although the monarchy was not abolished. It remained in place as a cultural symbol but did not have any real power. Under the new constitution, new civil liberties were granted to the population, such as freedom of speech.

Today, Japan is considered to be a developed country. Its population is well educated and affluent. Japan also boasts one of the most developed economies in the world. In a nutshell, the American occupation after the war can be seen as a huge success for both Japan and the West.

PART SIX:
The Cold War and the Space Race Begin (1945–1969)

Chapter 21: The Truman Years: The Cold War Begins

When the war ended, the US was the only nation that had managed to develop nuclear weapons, but the USSR was busy working. On August 29th, 1949, the Soviets were ready to test their first one. Seeing this, America created a program in 1950 dedicated to the development of nuclear weapons.

By this time, the United States was no longer actively practicing isolationism. Having played an integral role in ending the war, drafting the peace terms, and providing financial aid to the nations ravaged by war, it emerged as a global superpower. The USSR was also determined to assert itself as a superpower, which created conflicts between the two nations and ushered in the Cold War.

President Harry Truman

When FDR died unexpectedly weeks before Germany's surrender, Vice President Harry Truman became the new president. He carried the country through to the final end of the war and made the fateful decision to drop the atomic bombs on Japan.

While the terms of the peace treaty ending the war were being discussed, Truman was also working to improve America's social and economic state. On September 6th, 1945, Truman presented his 21-Point Plan to Congress. Under this plan, he proposed expanding the Social Security program, creating more public housing, and establishing the Fair Employment Practices Act, which FDR had created, as permanent legislation, among other things.

On the international front, one of the most significant policies to be implemented by Truman was the Truman Doctrine.

President Truman.
https://commons.wikimedia.org/wiki/File:Harry_S_Truman_-_NARA_-_530677_(2).jpg

In a bid to increase the reach of communism and its own influence, the Soviet Union looked at Greece and Turkey. The Soviets wanted to topple their governments and establish a communist regime. With this as the end goal, the Soviet Union supported communists within the countries during their civil wars.

During a joint session of Congress on March 12th, 1947, Truman spoke passionately about Greece's and Turkey's plight and asked for $400 million to help the two countries. He said it was imperative that the US help countries that were being threatened with terror by the Soviet Union. He was certain that if the US did not help the two countries, they would fall to communism. He felt America had an obligation to help countries be free and democratic.

This speech became known as the Truman Doctrine and was seen as an official declaration of the Cold War. Two months after the speech, Congress approved his request to send aid.

The doctrine was meant to counter Soviet communism expansion and officially changed America's stance on foreign policy by pledging to help any country that wanted to resist communism. With the Truman Doctrine, the US effectively moved away from its isolationist stance to take a more active role in international conflicts and events.

The argument didn't win over everyone, but it convinced most Americans that the Soviet Union and the spread of communism was a very real and horrifying threat. The Truman Doctrine set the stage for America's relationship with the Soviet Union for the next four decades.

Greek Civil War (1946-1949)

During the Second World War, the Axis powers occupied Greece from 1941 to 1944, leading to over 400,000 deaths and untold horrors. Greece's Jewish population was almost entirely exterminated. A year into the occupation, resistance groups began forming to fight back against the Axis.

The socialist National Liberation Front (EAM) was an alliance of a number of political parties and other organizations that fought for Greece's liberation from its occupation by the Axis. An anti-communist group called the National Republican Greek League (EDES), which received covert support and supplies from the British, fought against EAM. The exiled Greek government did not support EAM, while EDES did not support the exiled government.

The fear that the Soviets would install a communist regime in Greece was very real, and Churchill felt that Britain had to do something.

In September 1944, German troops finally began to leave occupied Greece. EAM sprang into action and, within months, had taken over most of Greece. On December 3rd, 1944, a violent and ferocious civil war erupted in Greece. Fighting between the communists and anti-communists, the latter of whom were supported by British forces, continued throughout the month.

By early January 1945, Britain launched an attack to seize Athens from enemy hands. Approximately 210 British troops died during the offensive, and hundreds more were wounded, but the attack was a success.

However, their victory was short-lived. The communists fought viciously. More than fifteen thousand Greeks and one thousand British civilians were captured by them. Many captives died.

As the war dragged on, Britain eventually pulled out from the fight in early 1947. But in 1948, following the Truman Doctrine, America stepped in and offered support to help the Greeks fight against the communists. This bolstered the Greek army. On October 16th, 1949, the communists declared a ceasefire, ending the civil war.

It was one of the earliest examples of America shifting its foreign policy and a foreshadowing of the types of roles it would continue to play in the future.

Another important policy that impacted America's role in the international world order was the Marshall Plan.

The Marshall Plan

Post-war Europe was left in utter shambles, with food shortages, diseases, and an unstable infrastructure. People were desperate, disheartened, and hungry. It was not outside the realm of possibility that these nations would turn to communism for help. The US realized one of the best ways of preventing it was to ensure European nations had economic stability and democracy.

On the heels of the Truman Doctrine, Secretary of State George Marshall delivered a speech on June 5th, 1947, which became the basis of the Marshall Plan. The plan, also known as the European Recovery Program, was simple: provide financial aid to nations in western Europe whose economies were left crippled by the war. By doing so, the plan's two goals would be achieved:

- The spread of communism across western Europe would be prevented.
- International stability would develop free-market economies and democracy.

The Marshall Plan was implemented in 1948. A total of sixteen nations in Europe received over $13 billion in aid through the plan. The money was not distributed equally. More money was given to industrial powers like Great Britain, which received approximately a quarter of the total aid, and France, which received one-fifth.

Countries like Italy, an ex-Axis power, received less. The one major exception was West Germany. With East Germany under complete Soviet control, it was imperative that West Germany's economy be revitalized and that the region become a democracy.

The Marshall Plan was deemed a resounding success, as it helped rehabilitate the shattered nations. By 1952, the economic growth in the sixteen nations that had received aid from the US exceeded pre-war levels.

For America, the plan also boosted its own economy, as more countries began trading with American companies. American interests in Europe were also firmly cemented, as some of the aid money was given to the Central Intelligence Agency (CIA) to establish businesses in European countries. These served as a front for America to gather information and further its own interests.

In short, a combination of the Truman Doctrine and the Marshall Plan ensured America's position in the world as a superpower.

North Atlantic Treaty Organization (NATO)

The Marshall Plan also acted as a catalyst for the creation of NATO.

While many European nations were in a better economic situation by the late 1940s and early 1950s, they didn't feel completely secure and safe. It became evident that some form of formal military cooperation would need to be established. So, some western European countries banded together and created the Western Union in 1948.

The North Atlantic Treaty Organization (NATO) was created in 1949 to defend the enlisted countries against any foreign threats. It came into existence with twelve founding countries:

- The United States
- The United Kingdom
- Canada
- France

- Belgium
- Denmark
- Italy
- Iceland
- The Netherlands
- Luxembourg
- Portugal
- Norway

The treaty was signed in Washington in early April of 1949, formally establishing Article 5, which essentially stated that if any member country was attacked, it would be seen as an attack on all the member countries. The members of NATO would have to retaliate. The main goal of the treaty was to safeguard NATO members' freedom and security through military and political assistance and to make sure Europe stayed at peace.

So far, Article 5 has only been invoked once, after 9/11. Today, membership in NATO has more than doubled, with thirty active members.

Given the fear of Soviet aggression, there were concerns the Western Union wasn't strong enough, so Truman made a proposal to Congress in 1949 to create the Mutual Defense Assistance Act. It was a military foreign aid legislation and would provide financial assistance to NATO countries. Congress signed off on it in October, and $1.4 billion dollars were set aside for it.

The United Nations

After the end of WWII, the world realized that it needed to develop friendly relationships and stay united to maintain international cooperation and global peace. This had been tried once before with the creation of the League of Nations. But lessons had been learned from the failed League of Nations, and the world was ready to try again.

The foundation of the League of Nations paved the way for the establishment of the United Nations. The United Nations was created after American President Franklin Roosevelt and British

Prime Minister Winston Churchill issued a declaration outlining a commitment to maintaining international peace. The declaration was signed by twenty-six countries, which all vowed to do the same. The United Nations was officially founded on October 24th, 1945, and was a reflection of how the US had taken on an international leadership role.

Over the years, the responsibilities of the UN have expanded to include helping developing countries find their footing socially, politically, and economically. Fifty-one nations initially joined the organization, but since then,142 more countries have joined, bringing up the number of member states to 193.

Chapter 22: The Ike Years: Coup d'états and Civil Rights

President Dwight D. Eisenhower

After Truman's second term as president ended, Dwight D. Eisenhower, an important military leader during World War II (he was the Supreme Commander of the Allied Expeditionary Force and a five-star general), won the election and took office. He revised America's national security policy so it would be more balanced, allowing the US to maintain its military commitments for the Cold War while keeping the country's finances in mind.

President Dwight D. Eisenhower.
https://commons.wikimedia.org/wiki/File:Dwight_D._Eisenhower,_White_House_photo_portrait,_February_1959.jpg

Eisenhower thought it was important to reduce government spending. Like Truman, Eisenhower also prioritized the elimination of communism and keeping it at bay. However, unlike Truman, Eisenhower was more focused on domestic issues, like the civil rights movement, rather than international relations. Eisenhower gave the CIA a lot of authority, particularly on matters outside of Europe. Two of the CIA's covert operations took down the Iranian and Guatemalan governments.

After becoming president, he ended the Korean War, which had started in June 1950 between North and South Korea.

The Korean War

After Japan surrendered in the Second World War, in August of 1945, Korea was divided in half along the 38th parallel by America and the Soviet Union.

With the Soviet Union rising as a possible power, it was crucial for the Allied powers to stop communism from advancing any further. So, while the Soviet forces set up camp and a communist regime in the north, the United States helped South Korea set up a military government.

Over the next five years, the two sides engaged in simmering tensions, which came to a head on June 25th, 1950, when North Korea invaded South Korea. The threat of the spread of communism was one of the major factors of the war.

North Korea was supported by the Soviet Union, which sent resources and equipment, and by China, which sent troops to fight in the war. Democratic Western nations sided with South Korea, although the bulk of the military assistance, aid, and troops were sent by the United States. During the three-year war, the US spent approximately $67 billion.

The Korean War ended up becoming a war of ideologies, as both sides fought to gain supremacy as the "real" Korea. The US was committed to helping South Korea resist communist expansion by North Korea. Negotiations for peace started in July 1951 and were finalized two years later.

An armistice was signed on July 27th, 1953, which means the war never officially ended (technically, it is still ongoing to this day). Around 2.5 million people died during the war. The war left the country destroyed and in shambles without resolving anything. Under the armistice, a demilitarized zone was established that ran along the length of the 38th parallel. But the two sides remained firmly divided and continue to be so.

Today, South Korea enjoys a strong economy and has a good support system in the international community with strong ties to democratic Western nations. Its people enjoy greater freedoms and a much better quality of life than the North Koreans.

The communist country has almost no ties with the outside world and continues to be ruled by one family. North Korea's economy is underdeveloped, and the people are cut off from the world and only given access to whatever the ruler wishes for them to have. North Korea's unpredictable behavior and desire to develop nuclear weapons pose a very serious threat to the United States and the world at large.

In some ways, Korea was just another casualty of the Cold War. The Korean War spun out of control, and it's far too late to reel the tensions back.

While Eisenhower didn't hesitate to spend money on defense, he was not keen on having American troops fight overseas, although military actions did take place. Eisenhower was also determined to improve the relationship with the Soviet Union, especially after Joseph Stalin's death on March 5th, 1953, which temporarily resulted in a thaw in the Cold War.

Cold War after Stalin

After Stalin's death, Nikita Khrushchev took over as head of the government and openly denounced Stalin's way of ruling and the crimes he perpetrated. After meeting with President Eisenhower in Geneva, Khrushchev expressed a desire for peace on both sides. The Soviet Union stated it would reduce the size of its military force by getting rid of over 600,000 troops.

His desire to get along is exactly what Eisenhower wanted as well. In September 1959, Khrushchev even visited the United States. But the relationship quickly started to get tense over Cuba.

Nikita Khrushchev

Bundesarchiv, Bild 183-B0628-0015-035 / Heinz Junge / CC-BY-SA 3.0, CC BY-SA 3.0 DE <https://creativecommons.org/licenses/by-sa/3.0/de/deed.en>, via Wikimedia Commons; https://commons.wikimedia.org/wiki/File:Bundesarchiv_Bild_183-B0628-0015-035,_Nikita_S._Chruschtschow.jpg

Fidel Castro, who took over in 1959 after finishing the Cuban Revolution, began to take steps that showed he was planning to make Cuba a communist country. This was something the US did not want, especially so close to its doorstep. Tens of thousands of Cubans fled, with many settling in Florida. When Eisenhower approved the overthrow of the Castro regime, Khrushchev warned him that Cuba would be protected by the Soviet Union through the use of nuclear missiles if needed.

After this, the tentative friendly relationship between the two leaders disintegrated, and America formally cut diplomatic ties with Cuba in 1961. Things further deteriorated when an American spy plane was shot down by the Soviet Union in 1960.

At home, Khrushchev's approach was more relaxed and less terrifying than Stalin's. Rules around censorship became more relaxed, the secret police was given less power, political prisoners were released, and the country even started to receive visitors. He launched the first satellite to orbit Earth, Sputnik, in 1957, kicking off the Space Race. In 1959, the Soviets crashed a rocket on the moon.

Khrushchev's approach emboldened eastern Europeans to seek greater freedom, but things went badly when Germans in East Berlin resisted increased working hours for the same wages. Violent riots broke out, leading three million Germans to flee to the West. To prevent any more people from leaving, Khrushchev authorized the building of the Berlin Wall in 1961, demonstrating he could be authoritarian when he wanted to.

The Space Race

At its core, the Cold War was a competition between two of the world's superpowers: the US and the Soviet Union. Each side wanted to prove it was the superior power, whether in politics, military, or technology. Everything was a race.

Like the arms race, space exploration was just another arena for the two competitors. Fueled by their desire to outpace the US, the Soviet Union launched Sputnik on October 4th, 1957. The artificial satellite would become the first manmade object to orbit Earth.

Replica of Sputnik 1.
https://en.wikipedia.org/wiki/File:Sputnik_asm.jpg

Unsurprisingly, the US was not happy about the launch of Sputnik. The American government felt as if the Soviet Union was overtaking them. Thus, the Space Race began.

The following year, Explorer I, a US satellite, was launched into space. In response to the launch of Sputnik, Eisenhower also signed an order on July 29th, 1958, authorizing the creation of a civilian agency called the National Aeronautics and Space Administration (NASA), which would be entirely dedicated to exploring space. The US and the Soviet Union each achieved some very important milestones, but perhaps the most important one was landing on the moon, which the US achieved in 1969. This will be discussed in further detail in the next chapter.

Rise of the Third World

While the Cold War was going on, there were many countries that chose not to align with either side. Those countries, the ones who were not a part of NATO or a part of the Warsaw Pact, were referred to as "Third World" countries.

On May 9th, 1955, NATO members decided to make West Germany a member and allowed the country to remilitarize. This was an obvious threat to the Soviet Union, which quickly drew up a treaty between itself and seven other European countries. It was signed in Warsaw on May 14th, 1955, and became known as the Warsaw Pact.

It was essentially the Soviet version of NATO's Article 5. Under the terms of the treaty, the countries that signed (Poland, Albania, Hungary, Romania, Czechoslovakia, Bulgaria, East Germany, and the Soviet Union) all agreed to defend each other if any of them was attacked by an enemy. The countries would band together and present a united front. Albania was expelled from the pact in 1962 because it started to question Nikita Khrushchev's policies. The pact remained in place until February 1991, when the Soviet Union started to dissolve.

The "First World" countries were developed Western nations like Canada, the United States, Japan, etc. Communist nations like China, North Korea, the Soviet Union, and Cuba were seen as "Second World" countries.

Most of the "Third World" countries had a colonial past and were struggling to recover from the atrocities committed against them. Over time, Third World became synonymous with countries in Asia, Africa, and Latin America. They were mostly considered to be underdeveloped because of a higher rate of poverty, disease, lower life expectancy, etc.

The terms were used to provide a broad political grouping of the countries around the world. Once the Cold War ended, the use of the term decreased and evolved. Today, we use terms like "developing countries."

American Society during the Cold War

As America embraced its role as a global superpower and exerted its influence on international conflicts and matters, domestically, the country was going through rapid social and economic changes.

Even though the Cold War was not an actual war (the Soviet Union and the US never directly fought each other), it still affected American society. Americans were terrified of communism and naturally distrustful of communists. This gave rise to McCarthyism, a political campaign that was based on the fear of communism in the United States. The campaign was spearheaded by Senator Joseph McCarthy. Many people who were accused or suspected of being communists were treated like the enemy in the US. They lost their jobs and were blacklisted.

The constant fear of a nuclear threat led to the creation of the National Defense Education Act and the interstate highway system. One of the common beliefs is that highways were built so that cities could be evacuated quicker in the event of a nuclear attack.

Defense or not, interstates changed the way Americans lived, ate, and socialized. New towns were built around interstate exits and grew rapidly. Small businesses and shops were replaced by motel chains and fast-food restaurants. The ease of traveling in and out of cities also led to more people moving away from the cities and settling into the suburbs.

Suburban life created a market for housing, grocery store chains, and new schools, parks, and other things. This, in turn, created new opportunities for jobs and industries.

Post-war America saw a huge boom in its economy, as trade with other countries increased dramatically. The production of goods and a strong economy led to the rise of consumer culture. Technological advancements in mass media helped advertise products and goods. Soon, people were recognizing brands and labels.

American society was becoming more modernized and more like the life we know today.

Civil Rights Movement

During the Progressive Era, most of the fight for social justice and reforms didn't really include black people. Even though Congress passed a few amendments, such as giving black men the right to vote, they were still not viewed as equals in society. Laws, like the Jim Crow laws, were established to segregate African Americans and keep them away from white society. However, some of the steps taken during the Progressive Era helped build the bridge toward a bigger movement in the 1950s and 1960s.

One of the catalysts for the civil rights movement was Rosa Parks. Rosa was a black woman who was sitting on a bus in a designated seat at the back of the bus, as per the segregation laws in Alabama. After some white passengers got on the bus and couldn't find a seat, the bus driver asked Parks and other African Americans sitting in her row to give their seats. Three of them moved; Rosa Parks refused.

Rosa Parks.
https://commons.wikimedia.org/wiki/File:Rosaparks.jpg

Because Rosa Parks refused the order, she was promptly arrested, which outraged the African American community and led to the creation of the Montgomery Improvement Association (MIA), which was led by Rev. Dr. Martin Luther King Jr. The MIA planned a boycott of the bus system, which lasted for over a year and led to the Supreme Court ruling that segregated seating went against the Constitution.

Although Eisenhower was the president when the civil rights movement began, Harry Truman was a great champion of civil rights. For instance, in 1948, he issued Executive Order 9981, which put an end to segregation in the Armed Forces. His views and stance on civil rights also made it easier for President Eisenhower to convince Congress of the need to write new civil rights legislation. The Civil Rights Act of 1957 was signed by Eisenhower, but blatant prejudice against black people continued.

Inspired by Gandhi, nonviolent protests by activists began to crop up around the country to protest against unfair laws like "whites only" lunch counters. As time passed, more radical groups were established, as not much seemed to be accomplished with peaceful protests.

During the 1960s, a group of activists made up of both black and white Americans called the Freedom Riders traveled to the South to protest against unfair segregation laws. They were treated horrifically by the police and white protestors. However, they also gained international attention, which put the world's focus on the civil rights movement in America.

Chapter 23: The Kennedys and the '60s: Dream up a Better World

American Culture in the 1960s

The foundation that was established in the 1950s for civil rights and other demands for social and political reform gained momentum in the 1960s, ushering in a tumultuous decade.

During the 18th and 19th centuries, several critical events, like the American Revolution, the Industrial Revolution, and the transcontinental railway, significantly altered the American landscape. The 1960s were also enormously important and peppered with profound events and movements that completely transformed America.

Some of the most notable events were the rise of the civil rights movement, the anti-war movement, multiple assassinations, and protests demanding reforms for social issues such as poverty, unemployment, and segregation. Feminists also actively fought for and demanded more equality. Society as a whole was moving toward a more liberal mindset, led in large part by baby boomers, who started the hippie movement in the late 1960s and early 1970s.

The name "baby boomers" was given to children born between 1946 and 1964; it was coined sometime in the early 1960s. In the

1960s, teenagers and young adults rejected the morals, values, and beliefs imposed upon them by their parents and society. The rejection of these traditions lay at the core of the hippie movement. People belonging to the movement adopted some distinct characteristics, such as long hair (for men and women), colorful tie-dye shirts, and flower crowns, to name a few.

The movement embraced the concept of free love and turned away from the idea of monogamy, preferring instead to live communally. They experimented sexually and were very open about love and sex, especially compared to the more conservative social mores in place at the time. Institutional religion was also rejected, and there was greater interest in religions like Buddhism. Drugs like LSD and marijuana were also used by many hippies. This type of free-flowing love, laid-back, easy way of living was reflected in the art and music of the decade.

While America was going through this profound social change, an extraordinary man named John F. Kennedy became the thirty-fifth president of America.

President John F. Kennedy

JFK was a remarkable leader who had big dreams for America. His vision of a united America included equal opportunities and human rights for all races, religions, and genders, which was perfectly aligned with the social reforms of the decade.

His time in office was unfortunately cut short, but within that limited time, he championed civil rights and helped the movement make great strides. He handled one of the worst Cold War crises with a cool head and diplomatic aplomb and inspired people to serve their country.

The Moon Landing

In the 1960s, the Space Race was well underway, and competition was heating up, especially with the establishment of NASA. Soon after JFK took office, one of his top priorities was the expansion of NASA and the space program.

In 1961, President Kennedy boldly declared that America would have a man on the moon before the end of the decade. His proclamation came true when, on July 20th, 1969, Apollo 11 landed on the moon. Astronaut Neil Armstrong walked on the moon, saying, "That's one small step for man, one giant leap for mankind."

An image of Buzz Aldrin on the moon.
https://en.wikipedia.org/wiki/File:Aldrin_Apollo_11_original.jpg

With the moon landing, America emerged as the clear winner of the Space Race with Russia. JFK did not live to see it happen, but he certainly pushed for space exploration while he was alive.

The Bay of Pigs

When it became clear to the United States that Fidel Castro was steering Cuba toward a communist regime, the administration decided it had to take action since his regime would be a threat to American interests.

As soon as Castro came into power in 1959, he started to implement policies that would reduce the amount of influence America had over the country. Industries like sugar, which had been dominated by the US for decades, were nationalized. He introduced land reforms and encouraged other countries in Latin America to become more autonomous and rely less on the US.

In response, the US decided to stop exporting sugar from Cuba, which would have been disastrous for the country's economy since 80 percent of its sugar went to America. To help Cuba out, the Soviet Union, which had already established diplomatic relations with Cuba, agreed to buy that share. These were things America did not want, so it began to carefully plot Castro's removal. In 1961, the US cut off all diplomatic ties with Cuba.

For the next two years, the CIA and the US State Department tried to remove Castro from power. They even recruited exiled Cubans who were living in Miami as part of their overthrow mission. However, they did not have much success.

With Kennedy's approval, on April 17th, 1961, the CIA and Cubans exiles launched a full-scale attack on Cuba. They were certain the invasion would be the definitive event that would get rid of him for good. But things did not go as planned, as it was a disaster almost from the start. Within a day of fighting, the vastly outnumbered American troops surrendered. Over 100 American troops died, and an additional 1,100 were captured.

Cuba would be the cause of tension once more during the Cuban Missile Crisis the following year.

The Cuban Missile Crisis

In October 1962, the Cold War reached new heights of tension when the US discovered that the Soviet Union had stationed nuclear missiles in Cuba.

After the Soviet Union's pledge to defend Cuba, Khrushchev started to store ballistic missiles in the country. Their proximity to the US was concerning because if they were launched, they had the potential to destroy huge swathes of the country.

The installations were discovered on October 14th, 1962, by a pilot flying an American U-2 spy plane. He took pictures and reported back. The following day, CIA analysts spotted missiles and launchers. Kennedy met advisors following this discovery to decide on the best course of action. An attack or war was out of the question for the president, so he settled on a naval quarantine to buy some time and figure out his next steps.

On October 23rd, Khrushchev replied to JFK's letter. He refused to remove the missiles, saying they were there purely for defensive reasons. Throughout the back and forth between the two leaders, the world held its breath, expecting nuclear weapons to go off at any minute. The threat of a nuclear war was a very real possibility.

War seemed imminent when, on October 27th, an American U-2 plane was shot down over Cuba. The pilot was killed. After some investigating, the US government concluded the order to shoot down the plane did not come from the Soviets. The incident made both sides realize just how dangerous things were becoming. It was clear neither side wanted war.

Thankfully, Khrushchev decided to remove the missiles, but he had some conditions. He wanted JFK to withdraw American missiles from Turkey and to stay out of Cuba. President Kennedy publicly agreed the US would not attack Cuba and also consented to take nuclear weapons out of Turkey.

Americans sighed a breath of relief on October 28th when Khrushchev wrote to JFK, agreeing to dismantle and remove the missiles from Cuba. The crisis and a potentially deadly war had been avoided.

Assassination of JFK

John F. Kennedy was an extraordinary president who ushered in a period of idealism and optimism, especially among the younger generation. As the youngest man to ever be elected president, he was a symbol of vigor and youthfulness and was viewed as "cool." His beautiful and elegant wife, Jackie, only added to his charm. When he was assassinated on November 22nd, 1963, it shocked the nation.

On the day of his assassination, he was driving in an open-top convertible with the governor of Dallas and his wife on a ten-mile motorcade through Dallas, Texas.

JFK motorcade.
https://en.wikipedia.org/wiki/File:JFK_limousine.png

Vice President Lyndon B. Johnson was also in the motorcade; he was several cars behind JFK.

At 12:30 p.m., three shots were fired, hitting President Kennedy and Governor John Connally. JFK died shortly afterward at Parkland Hospital in Dallas. Absolute chaos ensued, and Vice President Johnson was quickly sworn in as the thirty-sixth president on Air Force One.

That afternoon, a man named Lee Harvey Oswald was arrested for the murder of the president. On November 24th, when he was being taken to another county jail, he was swarmed by a crowd of people and killed by Jack Ruby as "revenge" for murdering JFK.

To this day, there are many conspiracy theories surrounding the Kennedy assassination and the real motive behind Ruby killing Oswald. Many believe he was killed to keep the truth about Kennedy's death hidden. Whatever the truth may be, the world and America lost an inspiring leader that day.

On November 25th, Kennedy was buried at Arlington National Cemetery with military honors. An eternal flame was lit by Jackie. It burned at his burial site until 1998 when it was moved to the National Museum of Funeral History.

JFK managed to leave behind a lasting legacy. He led the nation through part of the Cold War, albeit with some missteps. He fought to give Americans equal rights and encouraged people to take social and political action. He inspired an entire generation to do something for their country, their government, and the world by telling them during his inaugural address, "Ask not what your country can do for you—ask what you can do for your country."[7]

Vietnam War

During the Cold War, due to America's new foreign policy focused on containing communism, the US was actively involved in the war in Vietnam.

---

[7] "Ask Not What Your Country Can Do for You."
https://www.jfklibrary.org/learn/education/teachers/curricular-resources/elementary-school-curricular-resources/ask-not-what-your-country-can-do-for-you

After the French rule in Vietnam, which began in 1861 with the occupation of Saigon, came to an end on May 7th, 1954, the country was divided. War eventually broke out, lasting for two decades.

The divisive conflict began in 1954 with the Vietnamese movement to get rid of French colonial rule. It eventually evolved into a war between the communist government in North Vietnam against democratic South Vietnam.

American sympathy and support, of course, lay with South Vietnam, which fought against the Viet Cong (Vietnamese communists). The US was worried that if Vietnam fell to communism, other countries nearby would follow suit in a domino effect.

In 1961, Kennedy was advised to provide military, economic, and other aid to the South Vietnamese to help defeat the Viet Cong. While Kennedy increased the amount of aid, he didn't commit to a large military intervention. When the conflict started in 1955, there were less than eight hundred American troops in Vietnam, but by 1962, that number had jumped to nine thousand troops.

As the political instability increased in South Vietnam, President Lyndon B. Johnson, the man who replaced Kennedy after his assassination, agreed to increase military aid and support. By June 1965, eighty-two thousand American troops were in Vietnam.

American soldiers fought far from ideal conditions. They were fighting in unfamiliar, complicated terrain in a country fraught with political tensions and uncertainty. And worse, the American government didn't seem to have a clear motive or objective for the war, which seemed to drag on endlessly. Those taken as prisoners of war were subjected to psychological and physical abuse.

As the number of American casualties increased, people began to question what the US was actually doing in Vietnam. By the time the war ended, around 58,000 American soldiers had been killed, with another 300,000 wounded.

The media's portrayal of the war also turned public opinion against the fighting. Military personnel began to desert, and anti-war protests swept across the country, leading to violence, riots, and deaths. American involvement came to an end after Nixon became president and started to withdraw troops. The war would only end in the mid-1970s.

Kent State Shooting

The Vietnam War was a source of tension and conflict for the United States. The controversial war had left the country deeply divided. While most people believed the US was doing the right thing, a very vocal part of the US public was against American intervention in Vietnam. And as the war continued, more people turned against it. People took to the streets to protest the war and the military draft.

One of the reasons Nixon won the presidential election of 1968 was his promise to bring the war to an end. But two years later, on April 30th, 1970, instead of calling the troops back, Nixon gave permission to the armed forces to invade Cambodia, which was being used by communist Vietnamese soldiers to launch attacks in the south.

The tension surrounding the war came to a head following this decision. On May 1st, 1970, hundreds of students gathered together at the Kent State University campus and began to protest the invasion. They spoke out against Nixon and the war and clashed with the police.

At 11:00 a.m. on May 4th, approximately three thousand protesters, anti-war activists, and spectators arrived on campus to start a scheduled protest. Around one hundred Ohio National Guardsmen were also there, and they ordered the peaceful protesters to leave and disperse. Things quickly escalated and got out of hand, with the guardsman firing tear gas at the protesters and eventually firing into the crowd.

Four Kent State students were killed, and an additional nine were injured. To this day, it is not clear why the shots were fired or whether it was necessary. During court trials and investigations, the National Guard has maintained a firm stance that it was necessary.

The tragedy of the protest marked a turning point for the war, as it cemented the anti-war sentiments of the public. Some historians believe the Kent State shooting was partially responsible for Nixon's downfall.

Civil Rights Act

Martin Luther King

The civil rights movement, which had taken off in the 1950s, gained momentum in the 1960s. The movement was led by people like Martin Luther King Jr., Malcolm X, James Farmer, and many others. The figure most closely associated with the movement is likely Martin Luther King Jr.

King was the founder of the Southern Christian Leadership Conference (SCLC). He was a Baptist minister and a radical who challenged systemic racism. He was determined to gain equality, not just for African Americans but also for other people who came from disadvantaged backgrounds. He wanted freedom, human rights, and a universal income for all people, as it would enable them to maintain a basic standard of living. He fought for these things through peaceful means.

Martin Luther King Jr.
https://commons.wikimedia.org/wiki/File:Martin_Luther_King,_Jr..jpg

One of the earliest things he organized was the Montgomery bus boycott, which happened after Rosa Parks's arrest. He played a key role in the Memphis sanitation worker's strike, as well as the March on Washington, where he gave his famous "I Have a Dream" speech.

While many civil rights leaders in the 1950s and 1960s emphasized the need for nonviolent protests and passive resistance, protests by the general public were often anything but. There were also radical groups, like the Black Panthers, who believed that peaceful protests were not enough to get changes made at the highest level. Violent clashes and events and peaceful marches and protests dominated most of the decade.

But it wasn't all for nothing. The protests and the conflicts helped bring awareness to the plight of African Americans in the US and the need for equality. The fearless work done by the civil rights movement led to legislation like the Civil Rights Act and the Voting Rights Act.

Congress passed the Civil Rights Act in 1964. It prohibited anyone from being discriminated against because of the color of their skin, their race, their gender, or their religion. It was a huge victory for the civil rights movement since it meant, for the first time in US history, African Americans were treated as equals under the law throughout the country. Segregation was a thing of the past. It didn't get rid of racism, but it was still a big victory.

The Voting Rights Act, which was signed in 1965, was another monumental victory for the civil rights movement. Voting rights had been granted to African Americans in the Fourteenth and Fifteenth Amendments, but they weren't always enforced. Some state governments, especially in the South, made it difficult for minorities to vote. The new act expanded the protections and made it illegal to prevent someone from voting based on the color of their skin.

Why was this so important? Having the ability to vote means having a say in politics, which, in turn, forces political candidates to consider the well-being of all Americans, not just white people. It also allows people to serve on juries and have a say in what happens to one's peers who break the law. Today, the Voting Rights Act is seen as one of the most effective civil rights legislations to ever be produced by the federal government.

King played an instrumental role in some of these key pieces of legislation and was awarded the Nobel Peace Prize in 1964. He is also honored every year through a federal holiday called Martin Luther King Jr. Day.

Assassination of King

King's immense popularity continued in the mid-1960s. There were some African American youths who called for a more radical and confrontational way of forcing change, though. Their views were more aligned with those of Malcolm X, a black nationalist leader who scorned King's nonviolent approaches to the civil rights movement.

In response, King began to speak out publicly on other social issues that concerned all of America, like the war in Vietnam, unemployment, and poverty. As part of his work, King and other members of the SCLC went to Memphis, Tennessee, where sanitation workers were on strike. He gave a speech on the evening of April 3rd. The following evening, while he was standing on a balcony at the Lorraine Motel in Memphis, he was struck and killed by a sniper bullet that pierced his neck. He died in the hospital an hour later. He was just thirty-nine years old.

Shocked by the assassination, people took to the streets to protest. Violent riots erupted throughout the country. President Lyndon Johnson urged for peace. He pressured Congress to pass civil rights legislation, which was scheduled to be discussed by the House of Representatives. The Fair Housing Act, which prohibited any discrimination for buying or renting housing based on sex, race, or religion, was signed a few days later on April 11th.

James Earl Ray, the man suspected of killing Martin Luther King Jr., was caught on June 8th, 1968. He pled guilty, and the following year, on March 10th, 1969, he received a prison sentence of ninety-nine years. There were some doubts back then on whether he actually committed the murder or whether he was framed.

White and black Americans mourned King's death, yet it did not serve to bring them any closer. Instead, it created a greater divide between the two races. Many young blacks also used the assassination to become more radical, and his death led to increased support and participation in movements like the Black Panther Party and the Black Power movement.

Immigration and Nationality Act of 1965

Another significant piece of legislation that is worth mentioning is the Immigration and Nationality Act of 1965. In a deeply symbolic and poignant moment, President Johnson signed the act in front of the Statue of Liberty, which had been given to America as a gift from France as a symbol of America's freedom.

The act did get rid of the national origins quota system that the American government had been using for decades to control the number of immigrants who entered the country and where they came from. This opened up the opportunity for people all around the world to immigrate to America. Over the years, the country would become one of the most multicultural nations in the world.

Lyndon B. Johnson entered office with high ratings, but the violent protests and the Vietnam War made the people view him in a negative light. However, LBJ did a lot for the country. He introduced several major civil rights laws, established programs to aid the poor, created Medicare and Medicaid, and sought peace talks with the Soviet Union.

The Assassination of Bobby Kennedy

Another notable event to take place in the late 1960s was the assassination of Bobby Kennedy.

In 1967, Israel was engaged in a brief but vicious war against Syria, Jordan, and Egypt. Known as the Six-Day War, it was another battle in a string of conflicts between Israel and the Arabs that had started in 1948. The war was won by Israel, and it changed the map of the Middle East and led to tensions that exist to this day.

When Bobby Kennedy, JFK's younger brother, came out in public support of Israel, not everyone agreed with the sentiment or felt happy about it.

On June 5th, 1968, after having won the California presidential primary the day before, Bobby Kennedy was attending a campaign event at the Los Angeles Ambassador Hotel. Just after midnight, he was shot several times in the hotel corridor. The gunman was a young man of Palestinian origin named Sirhan Sirhan. Bobby was quickly rushed to the hospital, where he was pronounced dead the following day, on June 6th. He was forty-two years old.

Bobby Kennedy was devoted to fighting for civil rights and liberties and was widely admired by most of the American population, especially minorities. He was on the cusp of making great strides in politics and would have faced off against Nixon had he lived.

Sirhan was arrested immediately and confessed to shooting Bobby because of his support for Israel, a country that was actively oppressing Palestinians. In April 1969, he was sentenced to death for the assassination. However, he was never executed since the California State Supreme Court invalidated all death penalty sentences in 1972. As of this writing, Sirhan is still alive and is serving a life sentence.

Since Bobby's death, various conspiracy theories have surfaced about what actually happened that night at the Ambassador Hotel. Bobby's own son, Robert F. Kennedy, does not believe Sirhan killed his father. He has spoken out publicly about his belief that there was a second shooter responsible for Bobby's death. Whether this is true or not will likely never be known.

PART SEVEN:
Détente and the End of the Cold War (1968–1992)

Chapter 24: The Nixon-Ford Years: Détente and Economic Changes

Nixon-Ford years (1968–1976)

End of the Vietnam War

In 1969, when Republican President Richard Nixon was elected into office, he almost immediately began to withdraw American forces from Vietnam and began entering into negotiations for peace. The US, North Vietnam, and South Vietnam were involved in the negotiations, which stalled out and restarted several times over the course of three years. The Paris Peace Accords was signed on January 27th, 1973, and brought an end to the war in Vietnam.

Under the treaty, the US agreed to withdraw from Vietnam. In exchange, both sides would release their prisoners and would unite as one country peacefully.

Of course, nothing was achieved peacefully. As soon as the Americans left, the communists launched a full-scale attack. Two years later, they were victorious. The country reunified to form a communist regime on July 2nd, 1976. It became the Socialist Republic of Vietnam.

For the US, the war had been catastrophic; it would become the second-longest war the country had ever fought. Billions of dollars had been spent, and approximately sixty thousand lives had been lost, not to mention the decades of time and effort.

By the time the US finally pulled out of the war, over two million troops had served, and it had all been for nothing. Despite the government's best efforts, Vietnam fell to communism. However, the domino effect that the country feared did not happen; Laos is the only other Southeast Asian country today that is communist. As of this writing, Vietnam is one of five communist countries that still exist in the world.

SALT I Treaty

Through all this, the Cold War continued. As part of President Nixon's plan to bring an end to the war, he met with the president of the Soviet Union, Leonid Brezhnev, in Moscow, becoming the first US president to go to Moscow. After more than two years of discussions, the two leaders, who were eager to form a better relationship, signed SALT I (Strategic Arms Limitation Talks) in May 1972.

Under the agreement, both countries agreed to a maximum of two antiballistic missile (ABM) sites. An ABM is a missile that can annihilate an incoming missile. The second point was that they would not expand their inventory of intercontinental ballistic missiles and submarine-launched ballistic missiles to more than what they already had.

Even though there were many things SALT I did not touch or cover, it was seen as the beginning of a better relationship between the two countries.

This more conciliatory foreign policy became known as détente, and the Cold War thawed considerably, with the leaders visiting each other's countries and enjoying a friendlier relationship.

Oil Crisis of 1973

On the heels of the US pulling out of the Vietnam War, the country was faced with another crisis: oil.

The oil crisis of 1973 happened when the Organization of the Petroleum Exporting Countries (OPEC) decided to dramatically raise the price of oil. OPEC also prohibited the exportation of oil to a handful of countries, including those in western Europe and the United States, because they had supported Israel in its war against Egypt and Syria. Additionally, the value of the US dollar had been declining, thus decreasing OPEC's earnings.

The embargo deeply impacted American society. Factories were forced to cut back on hours, businesses placed restrictions on their opening hours, gas stations saw long queues, and the average American scaled back their lifestyle. Smaller cars became more popular, and people became more conscious of waste.

Negotiations between OPEC and the US took place during a summit in Washington. In March 1974, the embargo was officially lifted. But the ripple effects of the crisis would continue to affect the country for the better part of the 1970s.

The Nixon Shock

One of Nixon's objectives was to improve America's economic growth by providing stability in the workforce and the exchange rate of the dollar. He did so by implementing the "Nixon shock," the name given to a set of economic policies established by President Nixon. They were designed to do the following:

- Create better employment opportunities
- Help check the rising cost of living
- Protect the American dollar from international speculators

As part of the plan, Nixon issued Executive Order 11615, which gave tax cuts and put a freeze on any price increases or salaries for a period of three months. The policies were designed to help the American economy but, unfortunately, had the opposite effect. While the order is viewed as a political success, economically, it ended up being the catalyst for the dollar losing a third of its value and the stagflation that characterized the 1970s.

Stagflation is described as a period when economic growth slows or declines while unemployment and inflation rise. This was one of the ripple effects of the oil crisis, and unfortunately, Nixon's policies did not help the situation. Instead, they put an end to the Bretton Woods Agreement.

The Bretton Woods Agreement was established toward the end of the Second World War by the Allied nations to provide stability for international currencies. As part of the agreement, the International Monetary Fund (IMF) and the World Bank were created. The countries who joined the agreement promised to maintain a fixed exchange rate between the US dollar and their own currencies. This meant there was a currency peg to the American dollar that was based on the price of gold.

By establishing this agreement, countries were assured of a stable exchange rate, which was beneficial for post-war global reconstruction. It also created a better environment for fostering international trade.

However, one of the biggest flaws of the system was that in order for it to be successful, all involved countries had to coordinate their policies so the exchange rate would be aligned. After Nixon's policies were implemented, it resulted in the collapse of the Bretton Woods Agreement. However, the two key institutions that were created as part of it, the IMF and the World Bank, left a lasting impact on global currency and continue to play a pivotal role in international finance today.

The main goal of the IMF is to maintain stability in the international monetary system, which influences a country's trade, its investments, and its economy. The purpose of the World Bank is to provide support to underdeveloped countries. One of its main aims is to reduce poverty around the world.

Watergate Scandal

During Nixon's term as president, he accomplished several key things, such as laws to protect the environment, and his administration implemented a handful of important reforms, including *Roe v. Wade* and funding for Planned Parenthood. However, he is most commonly remembered as the only American president to resign because of a political scandal.

When Nixon was running for president again in 1972, there was a lot of tension in the country over the Vietnam War and other social issues. Nixon's advisors felt he needed to run a very aggressive campaign. The tactics soon tipped over into illegal activities, such as wiretapping.

The scandal officially began on June 17th when a few men were caught breaking into the office of the Democratic National

Committee's Watergate headquarters to steal documents and fix the wiretaps that were malfunctioning.

A security guard realized something was up and called the police. The intruders were apprehended. Upon their arrest, it was revealed the men were connected to Nixon and his reelection campaign. The shorthand for the campaign was CREEP (Committee to Re-elect the President).

Nixon tried very hard to cover up the crime, including publicly swearing to the American public that his administration had nothing to do with the break-in. Believing in his honesty, the American people once more voted him into office.

But the conspiracy was unearthed by two Washington Post reporters, Bob Woodward and Carl Bernstein, who were given the information anonymously by a source they referred to as Deep Throat. The most damaging piece of information that was revealed was Nixon's involvement and his attempt to bribe the burglars to keep them from talking. It was also revealed that Nixon had tried to convince the CIA to meddle in the FBI's investigation. This was a clear abuse of power.

As more and more of the conspiracy was uncovered and charges were laid out, Nixon's Vice President, Spiro T. Agnew, resigned from office in 1973. He was replaced by Gerald Ford. Less than a year later, on August 9th, 1974, President Nixon resigned. He was never impeached for what he had done, although the process had already begun by the time he resigned.

Upon his resignation, Ford, who was the minority leader of the House of Representatives, succeeded him and took office.

Gerald Ford

When Ford became president, the country was in dire straits. The US was in the middle of one of the worst economic crises seen in nearly half a century. Unemployment and inflation were rising sharply while the recession dragged on. The last time things were that bad in the country was during the Great Depression.

In addition to the economic challenges, the country was also undergoing a domestic energy crisis, which Ford couldn't do much about either.

After Nixon pulled out of Vietnam, North Vietnam's communist influence only grew stronger. Ford wanted to send American troops back into the country to help the South Vietnamese. But this request was flatly denied. So, he instead focused his efforts on reviving the policy of détente, which had been falling apart since the mid-1970s. The US organized the Conference on Security and Cooperation (CSCE) in Helsinki and discussed some critical issues surrounding the arms trade and human rights.

Ford's efforts came to fruition when the Helsinki Accords were signed by Canada, the Soviet Union, America, and all the European countries, with the exception of Albania, after the CSCE. Under the terms of the accord, the countries agreed to decrease tensions between the East and the West. The détente looked to be on the horizon once more.

However, concerns over the violation of human rights in Russia became the cause of dissent, and the policy of détente fell apart for the moment. Russia had been a one-party state with total control over its people since the start of the Cold War. The people of Russia were not afforded the same rights and freedoms as those of democratic nations, which was cause for concern to the West.

Nixon Pardon

Pardoning Nixon was perhaps Ford's most controversial act as president, and it is the thing for which he is most famous. After becoming president, one of the first things Ford did was pardon disgraced former President Richard Nixon for the role he played in the Watergate scandal.

Gerald R. Ford.
https://commons.wikimedia.org/wiki/File:Gerald_Ford_presidential_portrait_(cropped).jpg

The pardon meant Nixon was absolved of all criminal charges. This did not sit well with the American public, who felt the president should have been charged for his crimes and faced justice.

By the time the presidential election of 1976 rolled around, Ford was hugely unpopular, and he lost the election to Democrat Jimmy Carter by a significant margin.

With Ford and the Republicans out of office, the Nixon-Ford years officially came to an end.

Chapter 25: Jimmy Carter: The End of Détente

Carter's Domestic Policies

When Jimmy Carter was campaigning in 1976, one of his promises was changes to American foreign policy. As promised, after he was elected, American foreign policy shifted, with more of an emphasis on human rights.

Carter believed America had an obligation and moral duty to ensure human rights were adhered to and respected. It was an ideological shift for America, but Carter's administration was determined to "speak frankly about injustice, both at home and abroad" and take action as needed.[8]

President Carter believed that every human being had the right to the following:

- Be free from government violation
- Have basic necessities, like shelter, food, and an education
- Have civil and political rights

---

[8] "Carter and Human Rights, 1977–1980." https://history.state.gov/milestones/1977-1980/human-rights.

As such, throughout his political career, he prioritized education, health care, and the well-being of all Americans. While governor of Georgia, a position he held from 1971 to 1975, he pushed forward an education reform package called the Adequate Program for Education. He wanted to provide a better educational system by reducing the size of classes and ensuring that equal funding was provided to all schools.

Domestically, Carter's administration put a national energy policy in place to help conserve energy. He also encouraged looking into other resources as an alternative to oil.

While in office, he also pushed the Economic Stimulus Appropriations Act in Congress to help resolve the unemployment crisis. He believed the government's role should be to advance the common good, so the policies and acts he implemented were designed with that in mind. He wanted an open, transparent administration but faced a number of significant issues, including a Congress that wasn't entirely supportive of him.

Jimmy Carter was not like most politicians that Congress or Washington was familiar with. He was not happy to participate in back-door dealings or corruption. Carter was a reformer who believed in science and progress, and he had grown up with a strong faith and carried those values and morality with him. When he ran for office, he pledged to be an honest president who would lead the country by example and would never lie to his people. This type of personality was difficult for Congress to deal with, and there was simmering tension between Congress and the president since they had very different approaches to politics.

Carter and the Cold War

In regard to the Cold War, President Carter continued the work the previous presidents had started in trying to establish a better relationship with the Soviet Union.

China's relationship with America also improved greatly, and the two countries formally reestablished diplomatic ties in 1979 through a bilateral trade agreement, which led to significant financial gains for both countries.

In addition, Carter continued to hold additional discussions with the Soviet Union to expand SALT. But these talks fell apart and were put on hold in early 1980 after the Soviet Union invaded Afghanistan in December 1979.

The United States openly condemned the Soviet Union's invasion of Afghanistan. It not only soured the fragile relationship between the two countries, but it also ended the age of détente. President Carter wrote a letter to Brezhnev, making his displeasure clear and stating this aggression was not acceptable. Carter vowed to the American people that Middle East oil would be protected at all costs and would not be allowed to fall into Soviet hands. America put a trade embargo in place.

1980 Summer Olympics

In addition to putting SALT II on hold, President Carter also called for nations to boycott the 1980 Summer Olympics, which were scheduled to take place in Moscow, because of the Soviet invasion of Afghanistan. Following America's example, approximately sixty nations, including Japan, Canada, and most Arab countries, sat out the Olympics. However, some major western European players and American allies, such as France, Italy, and Great Britain, chose not to observe the boycott and sent their athletes to compete.

The Olympics were disastrous, with some countries protesting by refusing to attend ceremonies. Spectators were rowdy and rude, and the officials were clearly biased or even openly cheating.

Therefore, it was not surprising when Russia won a total of 195 medals, 80 of them gold.

Camp David Accords of 1978

One of Jimmy Carter's most astonishing feats as president was the peace agreement between Egypt and Israel, two countries that had waged wars on and off for nearly three decades.

Carter's original goal was to bring peace to the entire Middle East. As such, he wanted to invite countries like Jordan, Syria, and Palestine to the negotiating table. He felt peace in the Middle East would not only help improve America's relationship with the Soviet Union but also give the US a stronger foothold in the Middle East. But when it became clear that Egypt and Israel wanted to deal with just each other, Carter put his goal of a peaceful Middle East aside and focused on bettering the relationship between the two countries instead.

Egyptian President Anwar el-Sadat and Israeli Prime Minister Menachem Begin were keen to stay on friendlier terms since neither country felt very secure and was surrounded by enemies. Egypt was dealing with threats from Libya, while all the Arab countries around Israel refused to acknowledge its existence.

Despite their best intentions, negotiations stalled at multiple points. However, Carter refused to let it all be in vain and insisted on hosting both Sadat and Begin at Camp David. His administration, which was already dealing with an economic crisis and inflation, knew that to fail at this would be catastrophic. A tense two-week period followed, with the three leaders engaged in intense discussions.

The three leaders at Camp David.
https://commons.wikimedia.org/wiki/File:Camp_David,_Menachem_Begin,_Anwar_Sadat,_1978.jpg

Carter drew up a peace proposal and plainly stated that if they could not agree to terms, the US would withdraw aid money and its friendship. During this time, Carter put all his other duties on hold. He finally emerged from the talks on September 17th, 1978, with the news that peace had been agreed upon by Egypt and Israel.

It did not come without growing pains, and absolute peace was never fully achieved, but it was a positive step. To this day, the countries enjoy a cordial relationship. For Jimmy Carter, it was a diplomatic triumph.

Iranian Hostage Crisis (1979)

Within a year after the treaty was signed between Israel and Egypt, Carter faced a new crisis in the Middle East when Iranian students stormed the US Embassy in Tehran. To understand why, we have to go back several years.

Tensions between the US and Iran had been brewing for decades. The two countries often clashed over oil, as the majority of Iran's reserves were controlled by the US and Great Britain. Iranians were also unhappy with what they viewed as too much interference from the US in their domestic affairs.

In 1951, Mohammad Mossadegh was elected as prime minister of Iran. One of Mossadegh's top priorities was to nationalize Iran's oil. This was something America did not want, so the CIA and MI6 (Britain's intelligence service) hatched a plan to remove Mossadegh from power and replace him with someone of their own choosing. By August 1953, Mossadegh had been ousted, and a new government, headed by Mohammed Reza Shah Pahlavi, was established.

As an anti-communist, pro-West, and secular Muslim, Reza Shah was exactly what the Americans wanted. However, he made the Iranians miserable. Reza Shah was a brutal dictator who kept an iron grip on the country through his secret police (SAVAK), which tortured and killed thousands of people.

The Iranians were deeply resentful of the coup and of what the US had done to them. After nearly two decades of Reza Shah's rule, the people had had enough. Led by Ayatollah Khomeini, a radical Muslim, they forced Reza Shah and his government out. The US wisely stayed out of the revolution.

However, in 1979, when Jimmy Carter allowed Reza Shah to come to the US and receive treatment for his cancer, it was the final straw for many Iranians and became the catalyst for the protest in Tehran.

The pro-Ayatollah students forced their way into the embassy on November 4th, 1979, and took sixty-six hostages, many of whom were students, diplomats, and employees. Soon after, thirteen of the hostages were set free, with another being released a few months later. The remaining fifty-two hostages remained captives. While they were never seriously harmed, they lived in constant fear and were subjected to humiliating treatment.

In the meantime, the American government was working hard to set them free, but neither diplomacy nor economic sanctions could sway Ayatollah's stance. Releasing the hostages became a top priority for Carter, but his efforts were all in vain. As a result, he was viewed poorly by the American public.

His reelection campaign suffered greatly because of it. Ronald Reagan, his opponent, played this to his advantage. There were even rumors that Reagan's campaign team had made sure the hostages would stay in captivity until after the election so that Carter couldn't win.

Reagan staunchly denied these rumors and won the election in a landslide. In a curious turn of events, the remaining hostages were released on January 21st, 1981. hours after Regan made his inaugural speech.

Second Oil Crisis of 1979

The Iranian Revolution led to the United States going through a second oil crisis in the 1970s, which is also known as the 1979 Oil Shock.

As a result of the revolution, the global oil supply decreased, which led to the price of crude oil skyrocketing. Just like during the first oil crisis, the dramatic rise in prices led to fuel shortages and people cutting back on necessities.

President Carter encouraged Americans to try and reduce their consumption of energy. He even installed wood-burning stoves and solar panels on the White House roof to reduce energy usage. When Regan moved into the White House, he had them removed.

Things continued to get worse when the Iran-Iraq War began in 1980. Oil production fell sharply, leading to a global economic recession. It would take nearly half a decade for the prices to start going back to normal. Industries that relied heavily on oil began to look at other alternatives and made the switch from oil to other sources of power and energy, such as natural gas. Other countries, like Mexico, Venezuela, and the Soviet Union, began to expand their oil production, making the US less reliant on oil from the Middle East.

Chapter 26: Reagan and Reaganomics

After running a disastrous reelection campaign, Jimmy Carter lost the election to Republican candidate Ronald Reagan by a landslide. A former actor, Ronald Reagan was extremely popular with the public and was in office for two terms, serving from 1981 to 1989.

During his time as president, he achieved a number of significant things, such as getting the economy back on track, bringing an end to the Cold War, and appointing a woman to the US Supreme Court for the first time in history.

Reaganomics

Domestically, one of Reagan's main objectives was to fix the runaway economy. The economic policies implemented by Ronald Reagan are commonly referred to as Reaganomics. It was one of the most ambitious attempts at changing the country's economic policies since the days of the New Deal.

Reagan believed the key to growing the economy lay in reducing the government's growth. His Program for Economic Recovery, unveiled in 1981, was designed to reduce the cost of conducting business. This was achieved through tax cuts and relaxing price controls and regulations. He also aimed to reduce inflation by controlling the supply of money.

Because Reagan's views on government were that it should intervene less, life-saving government-funded programs, like Medicaid, Social Security, education programs, and food stamps, were the first to be cut. While he cut back on social spending, he increased military spending. By implementing these policies, he expected to reduce inflation and see a rise in investments and savings, which would ensure healthier markets and economic growth.

His policies had both negative and positive effects. Within two years, the economy began to recover. Reaganomics led to a period of prosperity and strong economic growth. For instance, the GDP improved by more than 25 percent, and inflation came down to 4 percent. Unemployment also dropped to 5.5 percent.

Reaganomics helped to reduce poverty, but it also increased social inequality by making the rich richer. His trickle-down economic policy resulted in high earners tripling their income, while low-income families only went up a few percentage points.

The War on Drugs

One of the most important federal legislations to be passed by the Reagan administration involved drugs. In October 1986, the Anti-Drug Abuse Act was passed and signed into law. Under the act, one billion dollars was committed to fighting the war on drugs, while the punishment for drug-related offenses became harsher. For example, if someone was caught with five grams of crack, they could be sentenced to a five-year prison sentence with no possibility of parole.

The act was partially inspired by Nancy Reagan's "Just Say No" campaign on drugs.

Nancy Reagan at a Just Say No rally.
https://commons.wikimedia.org/wiki/File:Photograph_of_Mrs._Reagan_speaking_at_a_%2 2Just_Say_No%22_Rally_in_Los_Angeles_-_NARA_-_198584.jpg

While the intent of the act and the campaign were done in good faith, there were a lot of negatives. The act did not take into account many socioeconomic factors or that addictions often occurred as a result of prescription medication.

In the long run, many believe Reagan's zero-tolerance policy did more harm than good, as it dramatically increased the number of incarcerations for nonviolent drug offenses, worsened racial inequality, and thrust mostly marginalized people into a cycle of violence and poverty.

Assassination Attempt

Soon after taking office, an attempt was made on President Reagan's life.

A man by the name of John Hinckley shot Reagan on March 30th, 1981, while the president was walking to his limousine after an engagement.

Six shots were fired by Hinckley, who was standing amongst a crowd of reporters. He was apprehended almost immediately. The president, who did not immediately realize he had been shot, was put in the limousine by his security detail and taken to the hospital. The bullet narrowly missed his heart and damaged his left lung instead. He underwent a two-hour surgery and was in stable condition. He even began working from the hospital bed the very next day.

Additional victims also recovered, although some suffered more serious injuries than others. James Brady, the White House press secretary, suffered permanent brain damage. The experience led to him becoming a staunch advocate of gun control.

As for Reagan, the assassination attempt raised his popularity even more.

Reagan and Foreign Affairs

Like his predecessors, Reagan and his administration continued to play a key role in international and foreign affairs, often acting as peacemakers.

When Israel invaded Lebanon in 1982, eight hundred US Marines were sent from the States on a peacekeeping mission to Lebanon. Over two hundred American lives were lost when suicide bombers attacked their barracks in Beirut.

In October 1983, on the heels of the losses in Lebanon, Reagan sent US forces to the island of Grenada after the Marxist government in Grenada launched a coup, killing the prime minister and seizing power. The American government authorized the invasion of Grenada to protect American nationals living on the Caribbean island. Many of these nationals were young medical students.

President Reagan had two thousand American troops sent to the island, and the invasion began on October 25th, 1983. Letting the rebels win would mean another communist government near the US, and Reagan couldn't have that. They met resistance from Grenada's armed forces and Cuban troops, which supported the Marxist government. An additional seven thousand troops were sent from the US. Within four days, the invasion was over, with the Americans coming out as the winners.

The Marxist government was toppled and replaced by one approved by the US. In total, twenty American soldiers were killed, and more than one hundred came back wounded.

Irangate

Reagan's administration did a lot of good for the country and the world; however, they were not entirely free from scandal. One of the biggest political scandals Reagan faced was Irangate or the Iran-Contra affair.

To understand Irangate, we have to go back to 1979 when Iran went through a revolution and overthrew its detested dictator, Reza Shah Pahlavi. Ayatollah Khomeini came to power and quickly created the Islamic Republic of Iran. His dislike for America and its influence on Iran was an open secret.

While Iran was going through its revolution, so was Nicaragua. In Nicaragua, a pro-Soviet group called the Sandinistas took over. Reagan, who was on a mission to eliminate communism, could not have this. He signed a secret order that gave the CIA the authority to provide the Contras—a paramilitary group working against the Sandinistas—money, weapons, equipment, and support. The end goal was to get rid of the Sandinista regime.

However, the money was provided covertly. America was illegally selling weapons and arms to Iran. The profit it made from these sales was secretly funneled to the Contras.

The illegal arms sale was revealed in a Lebanese newspaper while Regan was serving his second term. Reagan denied knowing anything about this but later retracted his words. An investigation, which would last for eight years, was launched.

Reagan was never charged with any crime or wrongdoing, and when his second term ended, Reagan was still very popular and beloved. Even today, his role in Irangate is often overlooked or sidestepped, so his legacy remains intact.

The *Challenger*

One of the more tragic domestic events that took place during Reagan's presidency was the Space Shuttle *Challenger* disaster, which occurred on January 28th, 1986.

Just after 11:30 a.m. that morning, the *Challenger*, which was carrying seven crew members and one civilian, began lift-off. Less than a minute and a half later, the shuttle broke apart and burst into flames. There were no survivors. Millions of students tuned in to watch a teacher ascend into space; instead, they watched as the *Challenger* fell back to earth in pieces.

This was the first major shuttle accident. The government launched an investigation to determine what went wrong. NASA was eventually able to figure out that one of the seals had malfunctioned as a result of the cold. For more than two years, while NASA worked on improving the space shuttles, no more astronauts were sent into space.

Escalation of Cold War

When Reagan became president, he also inherited the Cold War, which had been going on for decades.

After a period of relative stability and even the easing of tensions between the East and the West, things quickly began to deteriorate when the Soviet Union invaded Afghanistan in December 1979. The US strongly denounced this act, which led to an increase in hostilities and an escalation of the Cold War, sometimes referred to as the Second Cold War.

President Carter had placed embargos on Soviet imports, led a boycott of the 1980 Olympic Games, increased military spending, and provided money to Afghani rebels.

When Reagan replaced Carter, he continued in much the same vein, except he was far more aggressive. Reagan openly disliked communism and was determined to eliminate it entirely.

Anti-communist movements and rebels around the world began to receive secret funding from the US to help combat communism. His military spending increased because he invested heavily in troops and weapons as a precaution against the Soviet Union, which he viewed as an "evil empire."

As part of the Reagan Doctrine, financial aid was also provided to African and Latin American movements that rose up against communism.

The Strategic Defense Initiative (SDI) was put in place in 1983. The aim of the SDI was to develop weapons that would be based in space and could be launched at any minute to defend the US and counter any attacks from a Soviet missile.

The Strategic Defense Initiative ended in 1993. By the time President Clinton came into office, the Cold War was coming to an end, and the Soviet Union's nuclear weapons were also getting reduced. As a result, support for the SDI faltered.

In 1993, Clinton's administration ended the program and renamed the agency Ballistic Missile Defense Organization (BMDO). The agency fell under the Department of Defense and was responsible for the country's ballistic missile defense efforts. In 2002, BMDO was renamed the Missile Defense Agency (MDA).

Reagan also strengthened his ties with Western nations, such as the United Kingdom. Margaret Thatcher, the new prime minister of Great Britain, felt just as strongly about communism as Reagan and supported him.

The Second Cold War quickly became financially draining for the Soviet Union. When Mikhail Gorbachev became the leader of the Soviet Union in 1985, he felt the resources that were being poured into Cold War commitments could be better used to help Russia and its people.

Mikhail Gorbachev.
RIA Novosti archive, image #850809 / Vladimir Vyatkin / CC-BY-SA 3.0, CC BY-SA 3.0 <https://creativecommons.org/licenses/by-sa/3.0>, via Wikimedia Commons; https://commons.wikimedia.org/wiki/File:RIAN_archive_850809_General_Secretary_of_the_CPSU_CC_M._Gorbachev_(cropped).jpg

An agreement was signed by both countries in 1987. They agreed to get rid of intermediate-range nuclear missiles. Feeling emboldened by this historic progress, Reagan delivered a speech at the Berlin Wall and challenged Gorbachev to dismantle it.

The Berlin Wall, which had divided East and West Germany for many years, came down nearly two and a half years later on November 9th, 1989. When the Berlin Wall fell, it was viewed by many as a symbolic ending to the Cold War.

Reagan brought back a piece of the Berlin Wall with him to America. Today, it is displayed in Simi Valley, California, at the Ronald Reagan Presidential Library.

Chapter 27: George H. W. Bush: The End of the Cold War

After Ronald Reagan's second term ended, the Republicans stayed in power, with George H. W. Bush taking office as the forty-first president of the country. He was inaugurated on January 20th, 1989, and was the sitting president when the Berlin Wall actually fell.

Reunification of Germany (1990)

The reunification of Germany began on November 9th, 1989, when East Berlin's Communist Party announced that citizens would be free to cross the borders. On the first weekend after this announcement was made, droves of people from East Berlin made their way into West Berlin to celebrate and reunite with friends and family. People soon began to break down pieces of the wall until the whole thing came down.

People stand on top of the fallen Berlin Wall.
Lear 21 at English Wikipedia, CC BY-SA 3.0 <https://creativecommons.org/licenses/by-sa/3.0>, via Wikimedia Commons; https://commons.wikimedia.org/wiki/File:West_and_East_Germans_at_the_Brandenburg_Gate_in_1989.jpg

The Cold War did not automatically end with the fall of the Berlin Wall, nor did it lead to a unified Germany. The reunification of Germany took months and happened officially on October 3rd, 1990, nearly a year after the Berlin Wall came down.

Malta Summit

While Reagan was president, he started to develop a friendship of sorts with Mikhail Gorbachev, who was also keen on having a better relationship with the West. After Bush took office, he was, at first, hesitant and wary of the Soviet Union, but after some time, he continued the efforts Reagan had made and opened up a dialogue with Gorbachev.

The two leaders decided to meet in Malta to continue their conversations in person. While a formal treaty was not discussed, Bush did allude that US policies toward the Soviet Union might change as their relationship evolved.

The Malta Summit took place on warships that were anchored in the Mediterranean between December 2nd and 3rd, 1989. During the summit, Gorbachev made it clear they were ready to leave the Cold War behind and start fresh.

By this time, a number of communist bloc governments had begun to collapse, including Bulgaria, Poland, and East Germany. The Soviet Union didn't try to resist or intervene in any of these countries. This acceptance was a dramatic change in outlook from four decades ago.

Another shocking shift was the Soviet Union's foreign minister's visit to NATO headquarters. After his visit with NATO Secretary General Manfred Wörner, he stated that he felt the Cold War was over. Gorbachev hoped the East and the West would find a way to end the decades-long confrontation and start building toward cooperation.

START Treaty (1991)

The START Treaty (Strategic Arms Reduction Treaty) had initially been proposed by President Reagan as part of disarmament talks that started in the early 1980s. These discussions continued between President Bush and Soviet leader Gorbachev.

START was signed on July 31", 1991, by both leaders. Under the terms of the treaty, both countries were limited to the number of nuclear warheads and Intercontinental Ballistic Missiles (ICBMs) they could have. After the treaty was implemented, approximately 80 percent of the strategic nuclear weapons possessed by the US and the Soviet Union were removed, destroyed, or deactivated.

The START Treaty was ratified in Congress the following year in October. It was one more step toward bringing an end to the Cold War.

Dismantling of the Soviet Union

After decades of iron control, the Soviet Union was beginning to lose the grip it once had on Eastern Europe. The Soviet Bloc began to unravel in 1989 when Poland elected a non-communist government. When the Soviet Union did nothing, other countries began to follow suit like dominoes, clamoring for freedom.

One by one, through peaceful revolutions, communist regimes in Hungary, Czechoslovakia, Romania, Bulgaria, and Albania were all ousted and replaced by non-communist governments. Latvia, Lithuania, and Estonia, the three Baltic states, also declared their independence from the Soviet Union.

End of the Cold War

The Cold War didn't formally end in any type of dramatic way; instead, it was a series of events that started during the 1980s that culminated to a point where there was no more Cold War and no more Soviet Union.

Gorbachev heavily influenced the last phase of the Cold War, and he is credited with ending it peacefully and without shedding blood. Not an easy feat for a country that saw communism take over in a bloody way. His radical reforms, policies, and redirecting of resources prioritized the growth of the country and the people. The easing of tensions and the more relaxed approach eventually led to the fall of the Berlin Wall and the Soviet Bloc.

By the end of 1991, as more countries moved away from communism, it was clear the Soviet Union was going to collapse. On December 25th, 1991, he resigned, saying, "We're now living in a new world. An end has been put to the Cold War and to the arms race."[9] Boris Yeltsin took over, and on December 26th, 1991, the Soviet Union was officially dissolved.

For his role in helping to end the war, Gorbachev won a Nobel Peace Prize on October 15th, 1990.

First Gulf War (1990-1991)

As the Cold War began to end, another international crisis was looming that would result in American intervention. The leader of Iraq, Saddam Hussein, had been eyeing oil-rich Kuwait for some time. Tensions between the two countries had been brewing for years.

On August 2nd, 1990, Saddam decided to invade the country. He hoped to gain control of the large oil reserves in Kuwait, get out of paying the debt Iraq owed to Kuwait, and expand his power and control in the region.

---

[9] "Collapse of the Soviet Union." https://www.history.com/topics/cold-war/fall-of-soviet-union.

The Kuwaitis actively resisted and fought back against Iraqi forces, but it did not go well. Over the span of 14 hours, around 4,200 Kuwaitis were killed. Over the next few days, Iraqi forces easily and quickly took over Kuwait City. Members of the royal family of Kuwait and hundreds of thousands of Kuwaitis fled the country and took refuge in nearby Saudi Arabia.

By the end of August, Saddam boldly declared that annexed Kuwait was now a part of Iraq as its nineteenth province. Iraqi troops occupied the country and wreaked a campaign of terror on the Kuwaitis, raping, torturing, and killing as they pleased.

Given how protective the West has always been over oil in the Middle East, nations acted swiftly. Within days of the invasion, the United Nations Security Council banned trade with Iraq. In the meantime, American troops were sent to Saudi Arabia.

The Arab League also spoke up and condemned the invasion and supported the UN's resolution. Some Arab countries, like Jordan and Tunisia, were sympathetic to Iraq and took Saddam's side.

In a surprising turn of events, the Soviet Union also came forward to support America. All in all, the invasion was shaping up to be a significant international crisis. It was the first one in a post-Cold War world.

Kuwait was also home to more than 600,000 expats, nearly 10,000 of which were Western nationals. They were all trapped in the country and forbidden from leaving by the Iraqi regime. Westerners soon began to be rounded up by Iraqi troops to be used as shields in case of an attack by the West. Saddam declared that children and women would be allowed to leave, but the situation was too tense and unpredictable. It seemed quite likely he would attempt an invasion of Saudi Arabia next, which would put 40 percent of the world's oil in his control.

America began to plan its overseas deployment, the largest one since WWII. By the end of November 1990, close to half a million US troops were stationed in the Gulf. Additional troops from the UK, Canada, Bangladesh, and France, to name a few nations, also arrived.

All the while, the UN was debating whether the use of force could be sanctioned if Iraq did not comply and leave Kuwait by a specified date (January 15th, 1991). The council decided that it would use "any means necessary" to remove him after that date.

Operation Desert Storm

Saddam, of course, refused to withdraw, and on January 17th, 1991, President Bush gave the go-ahead for American troops to attack Saddam's army. The mission's goal was to get rid of the Iraqi forces that were occupying Kuwait. The campaign consisted of a military coalition of thirty-five countries and began with aerial bombing. The war lasted for forty-two days and consisted of operations on both ground and air.

Oil wells on fire during Operation Desert Storm.
https://commons.wikimedia.org/wiki/File:Operation_Desert_Storm_22.jpg

Saddam's forces were successfully pushed out of Kuwait, and after a heavy bombing campaign on Baghdad, Iraqi troops began to surrender. On February 28th, a ceasefire was declared. Bush had successfully managed to roll back the invasion of Kuwait by Iraq.

NAFTA (1992)

The North American Free Trade Agreement (NAFTA) was established as a way to stimulate trade with participating countries, reduce costs, increase production, create new jobs, and bring prosperity. It was partially inspired by a similar trade agreement that had been created in Europe called the European Economic

Community in 1957. The US felt an agreement like this would also help North America gain a more competitive footing globally.

NAFTA was signed in 1992 by American President George H. W. Bush, Mexican President Carlos Salinas de Gortari, and Canadian Prime Minister Brian Mulroney. It was slated to take effect on January 1st, 1994.

With the signing of NAFTA, tariffs on most of the goods produced by the three countries were lifted. In some ways, NAFTA was a positive thing. It did help attract foreign investments and lower the cost of goods, which benefited the consumer. It also increased trade. But in other ways, it had a negative impact on the American economy, as many manufacturing jobs were relocated to Mexico, where labor and the cost of operating a business were cheaper. It affected smaller businesses and farms in Mexico, which couldn't lower their costs enough.

PART EIGHT: From Clinton to Trump (1992–2021)

Chapter 28: The Clinton Years: The Swift and Scandalous '90s

During the presidential election of 1992, Bush ran for reelection but was defeated by Democratic nominee Bill Clinton.

President Bill Clinton.
https://commons.wikimedia.org/wiki/File:Bill_Clinton.jpg

Clinton would go on to serve two terms in office. His presidency is generally viewed as an easy time for America. International conflicts and events were still taking place, but they were nothing like the tension-filled Cold War years.

By the time the '90s rolled around, America had really found its footing, both at home and globally. It was the decade when the fruits of past labors could be enjoyed. Hard-won freedoms by civil rights activists, women's groups, and other reformers had all allowed for the progressive, modern, diverse, and advanced society that America was in the 1990s.

Clinton's Domestic Policies

When Clinton was campaigning, he promised to tackle important social issues like unemployment, health care, and the economy. During his presidency, he implemented many domestic policies and legislations to help address and advance those issues.

Within his first year in office, Clinton passed an economic package called the Omnibus Budget Reconciliation Act of 1993. Under this act, the federal income tax for the upper class went up from 31 percent to 39.6 percent. The corporate tax rate went up, while government spending was cut by $255 billion over a period of five years. This negatively affected struggling Americans, who relied on many of the programs the government was cutting.

Although it was not popular with Republicans, Clinton's economic policy brought the government's deficit down from $290 billion to $203 billion in a matter of two years. And by the end of the 1990s, the economy was not only booming but also had a surplus of over $120 billion. A combination of low inflation, low interest rates, and low unemployment rates made the American economy one of the strongest and most enviable in the world.

Clinton also fulfilled another campaign promise by passing a sweeping reform bill on welfare assistance. He increased the minimum wage to $5.15 an hour.

At this point in American history, gay men and lesbians were excluded from the military. Clinton vowed to change this. A bitter political fight ensued with conservative individuals in the military. Congress eventually forced Clinton to reach a compromise. He proposed the "don't ask, don't tell" policy. If military personnel didn't ask about someone's sexual orientation, they wouldn't need to discuss it. It wasn't a perfect solution, but it was something.

On February 5th, 1993, Clinton signed the Family Medical Leave Act into law. The law granted workers family and medical leave of up to twelve weeks if the need arose. The leave was unpaid, but the act ensured their jobs would be protected and that their health insurance would be unaffected.

One of the things Clinton failed to do, something that was very close to his heart and important to him, was provide affordable health care for all Americans. While Clinton was running for office, there was a great deal of chatter and interest surrounding health care reform. Today, the US and South Africa are the only developed nations that do not provide universal health care for their people. Back in the 1990s, Clinton wanted to change this. Socially, it would be life-changing for Americans, and politically, it would ensure that the majority of the middle- and working-class population would align themselves with the Democrats.

The Republicans were fiercely determined not to let this happen and strongly objected to a health reform bill.

After Clinton took office, he created a task force to develop a proposal. His wife, Hillary, was put in charge of drafting the bill. The final product, a 1,350-page proposal, was difficult to understand for the average public, and it never got off the ground.

There are a few reasons why the health care reform failed. Firstly, Clinton presented it to the Senate after budget discussions had already been completed instead of beforehand. Thus, it should have been no surprise when the Senate did not approve the proposal. In the Senate's view, it would cost too much money, and the coverage provided to Americans was too extensive.

The administration's unwillingness to compromise on it made matters worse. The general consensus was that the proposal was too radical. By the time a task force did start to look at some compromises, the momentum was lost, and the reform ultimately failed and was shelved.

To this day, universal health care and gun control remain hotly contested and deeply divisive issues in America.

Columbine High School

Around 11:19 a.m., on April 20th, 1999, two teenagers armed with guns went to Columbine High School in the suburbs of Denver and started shooting at students outside the school. Then, they went inside the school and gunned down more students.

By 11:35 a.m., thirteen people had been killed: twelve students and one teacher. An additional twenty-one people were left wounded and injured. Just past noon, the teens killed themselves, bringing an end to their shocking and senseless killing spree.

Although Columbine was not the first school shooting in America, the public was left devastated and outraged that something like this had taken place. It affected Clinton on a deeper level, and the way he handled the tragedy set a precedent for how future presidents should behave and led to the examination of how presidential roles have evolved over time.

After the Columbine shooting, Clinton visited the victims' families. He comforted them, listened to them, and played the role of "Counselor in Chief." It was a break from the often-stoic attitude of past presidents who kept their emotions in check.

Following the shooting, Clinton advocated for stricter gun control but was not successful in getting anywhere. Gun control is a divisive topic in US politics today, and school shootings, as well as other mass shootings, still remain a problem.

Clinton's Foreign Policies

When Clinton became president, he wasn't very experienced in foreign affairs or policy. He came to power at a very interesting time. The Cold War had ended, and the Soviet Union had collapsed; it was almost like a new world.

Clinton swiftly understood the importance of globalization and saw it as a way of developing international relationships, enjoying shared prosperity, and promoting peace. He believed American foreign policy should be designed for the global age and that it must constantly evolve and adapt to keep up with the changing times.

In 1993, he welcomed new members into NATO, allowing it to evolve from Cold War alliances to include new friendships and partnerships. Russia was brought into the G-8, and Russian troops were even used to help NATO missions.

Clinton reduced tensions with North Korea through diplomacy and, in 1994, even managed to negotiate an agreement with the country to dismantle nuclear weapons. He also worked hard to create stronger bonds with South Korea.

In short, he tried to create a more inclusive global environment. We will take a closer look at some of the more notable international events and conflicts that took place during Clinton's presidency, although, like most topics in this book, this only scratches the surface of what happened during his presidency.

War in Bosnia

The Bosnian War began with the break-up of the Socialist Federal Republic of Yugoslavia, which included Croatia, Bosnia-Herzegovina, Serbia, Slovenia, Macedonia, and Montenegro. As the Soviet Bloc began to collapse, the six republics within Yugoslavia began to also divide based on their ethnicity.

In June 1991, Slovenia and Croatia declared independence. Less than a year later, Bosnia-Herzegovina also stated its intention to separate. It officially became independent on March 1st, 1992, which became the catalyst for the war.

Using the crisis to their advantage, Bosnian Serbs, with the help of Serbia, set out on a campaign to ethnically cleanse the country of Bosniaks or Bosnian Muslims. Their end goal was to wipe out the Muslim population and create a state free of Bosniaks. They began their offensive by bombing and seizing Bosnia's capital, Sarajevo. Bosnian Muslims fled by the thousands.

The genocide in Bosnia took nearly 100,000 civilian lives, most of which were Bosniaks. More than two million people were displaced, and up to fifty thousand women were subjected to rape, violence, and other brutalities. Thousands of others went missing, never to be found again.

At first, the UN and the US refused to intervene until the summer of 1995, when Bosnian Serbs killed eight thousand men and boys in Srebrenica within ten days. Srebrenica had been designated by the UN as a safe refuge. Between twenty-five thousand and thirty thousand women and children were abused and/or forced to move to other Muslim areas. Some of them got on buses and were never seen again.

It was at this point that Clinton decided that something had to be done. He put Operation Deliberate Force in motion. NATO led air strikes, launched an offensive in Croatia, and intervened in the war.

The Clinton administration negotiated the peace treaty. The Dayton Agreement, which was signed by Bosnia, Serbia, and Croatia in 1995, brought the long and bloody war to an end. According to the treaty, Bosnia would remain a single state but have two parts: the Federation of Bosnia and Herzegovina, which was mostly populated by Croat-Bosniaks, and the Republika Srpska, which was mostly populated by Serbians. The capital city, Sarajevo, stayed undivided.

American intervention and the subsequent peace treaty served to showcase America's prowess on the international scene and Clinton's negotiation skills and diplomacy. The agreement still stands today and is used in the governing structure of Bosnia and Herzegovina.

The way Bosnia was handled also provided a precedent for what would happen in Kosovo around four years later.

Kosovo Conflict

Three years after the war in Bosnia ended, ethnic Albanians were fighting against Serbs and the Yugoslavian government in Kosovo. After Slovenia and Croatia declared independence, ethnic Albanians in the Federal Republic of Yugoslavia decided to also separate and create their own republic called Kosovo. The crisis led to another round of ethnic cleansing by Yugoslavia, as Yugoslav soldiers, mainly Serbians, drove Albanians out of the country or had them killed.

Having witnessed the war in Bosnia, this time, the international world was determined not to sit on the sidelines. A national emergency was declared by Clinton on June 9th, 1998, and NATO intervened shortly after launching Operation Allied Force.

NATO and American forces began air strikes, targeting government buildings and other infrastructures in Yugoslavia. After enduring eleven weeks of bombing, Yugoslav forces withdrew from Kosovo.

The Kumanovo Treaty was signed on June 9th, 1999, with the Yugoslavian government agreeing to withdraw after NATO forces did. After the Yugoslavs left, NATO troops came into Kosovo to begin a peace support mission.

In both these examples, we can see how Clinton and America took charge; they decided on a course of action and followed through with it. There was no questioning America's authority or superiority as a global power in the 1990s.

Clinton-Lewinsky Scandal

Finally, no chapter on Clinton can be complete without bringing up his affair with Monica Lewinsky. The political sex scandal rocked the nation and is still widely discussed and talked about today.

During the summer of 1995, recent college graduate Monica Lewinsky started working at the White House as an intern in the office of the chief of staff. A few months later, in the fall, she was moved to the West Wing, along with a few other interns, for basic administrative duties. This brought her into contact with Clinton, who was very taken by the beautiful, young Lewinsky.

Monica and President Bill Clinton.
https://commons.wikimedia.org/wiki/File:Bill_Clinton_and_Monica_Lewinsky_on_February_28,_1997_A3c06420664168d9466c84c3c31ccc2f.jpg

Monica herself was quite smitten with the president. The two quickly became involved and continued to meet and have sexual encounters, even after Monica took a job in another office. By 1997, they stopped their sexual trysts and mostly kept in touch over the phone.

The affair came to light after Monica confided in a friend and coworker named Linda Tripp, who betrayed Monica by telling the story to a literary agent and secretly recording their phone calls. In the meantime, Kenneth Starr, an independent counsel who was looking into Bill and Hillary's investments in a business venture, stumbled onto the scandal. The story quickly took on a life of its own, and the scandal erupted. Americans were both shocked and fascinated.

At first, Clinton denied the affair, but when a blue dress worn by Monica with semen stains on it came to light, he backtracked. Clinton later admitted to a grand jury that he had, in fact, engaged in inappropriate behavior with Lewinsky. He publicly apologized for his behavior.

In October 1998, the House of Representatives moved to impeach him. At Clinton's trial in February 1999, he was acquitted. Although Clinton had clearly broken the trust of the American public, he finished his term as president while maintaining strong ratings.

The scandal might have shocked the country, but it did not lessen many people's admiration or devotion to Clinton. However, Hillary faced a lot of criticism for standing by his side. Lewinsky was publicly shamed and bullied. The stigma of the affair clung to her for decades. In 2016, when Hillary Clinton ran for president against Donald Trump, the scandal was dredged up again and used against her in smear campaigns.

Despite doing a lot of good and leaving behind quite a legacy, Clinton's presidency will always be marked by the Lewinsky affair.

Chapter 29:
The George W. Bush Years: 9/11 and the War on Terror

If Clinton's time in office was easy, smooth, and tension-free, George W. Bush's presidency was the exact opposite. His presidency started badly almost from the very beginning, starting with the election itself.

The race for the presidency between him and Democratic nominee Al Gore had been a tight one. By the time election day was coming to an end on November 7th, 2000, it wasn't really clear who the winner was. The race in some states, such as New Mexico and Oregon, was too close to call and stayed that way for days.

Eventually, Florida became the focus of the presidential election results, with some networks announcing that Al Gore was the projected winner. This was reversed later, with Bush being declared the winner. Al Gore called Bush on November 8th to congratulate him and concede. However, by the next morning, it was discovered that only a few hundred votes separated Bush and Gore, putting the margin of victory at around 0.1 percent. Al Gore called Bush again to rescind his concession.

Legal teams from both parties went to Florida, and a machine recount took place, which put Bush ahead of Gore by just over three hundred votes. But other legal issues and questions continued to plague Bush's win, which continued to be contested. The case was taken all the way to the US Supreme Court, where the decision was made to terminate the recounting process. The twenty-five electoral votes in Florida were given to Bush, cinching his win. Bush was inaugurated as the forty-third president on January 20th, 2001.

When Bush left office, his approval rating hovered somewhere in the twenties. His administration was excessive, and he was not a stellar leader. Therefore, he was woefully underprepared for the events to come.

9/11

About eight months after Bush took office, the United States was attacked by terrorists. On September 11th, 2001, between the hours of 7:59 a.m. to 8:42 a.m., four passenger planes took off. Two planes were from Boston, Massachusetts, one was from Washington, DC, and a fourth took from Newark, New Jersey. The flights were all headed to the same place: California. What none of the passengers could have known was that terrorists with links to al-Qaeda were sitting among them.

The four planes were hijacked. They never made it to their destination. Instead, two of the planes headed for New York City and crashed into the Twin Towers of the World Trade Center. The first plane hit the North Tower at 8:46 a.m.; the second one crashed into the South Tower at 9:03 a.m.

Twin Towers burning.
Michael Foran, CC BY 2.0 <https://creativecommons.org/licenses/by/2.0>, via Wikimedia Commons; https://commons.wikimedia.org/wiki/File:WTC_smoking_on_9-11.jpeg

The third plane crashed into the Pentagon at 9:45 a.m., while the fourth plane, which was likely meant to target the White House or the Capitol, crashed in a field in western Pennsylvania because the passengers fought back.

The attacks are commonly referred to as 9/11. A total of 2,996 people died during the attacks, with thousands of others sustaining injuries. Most of the victims were from the World Trade Center.

Americans were shocked, then grief-stricken, and then enraged by the attacks. All eyes were now on Bush.

Global War on Terrorism

Following 9/11, Bush had one goal in mind: to defeat terrorism. He soon launched a campaign called the Global War on Terror. One of the first things he did was freeze the assets of any groups linked to terrorist activities while demanding that the Taliban stop protecting al-Qaeda members.

By early October, he was planning for military strikes in Afghanistan against al-Qaeda. He planned for the American military to also provide aid to those in need in Afghanistan.

The invasion of Afghanistan by American and Allied troops happened within a month of the 9/11 attacks. Bush saw it as an act of self-defense. His target was the Taliban regime since it had provided a safe haven for al-Qaeda.

During the early days of the war, the US carried out air strikes. After losing some key players, the Taliban regime began to crumble, although it didn't remain that way for long. The Taliban regrouped. For the next two decades, things continued in this fashion, with each side gaining a little and then losing a little.

Afghanistan became the longest war that America had ever fought. When US troops finally left in 2021, it became clear the US had lost the war.

War in Iraq

While trying to root out al-Qaeda, Bush began to put pressure on Saddam Hussein for a number of things, including his ties with terrorists and his weapons of mass destruction. Saddam, of course, refused to cut ties or dismantle the weapons. By March 2003, Bush decided that Saddam had to go, and military operations were put in place for that purpose.

The official reason provided by the Bush administration for the invasion of Iraq was to disarm the country, root out al-Qaeda, and free the Iraqi people from Saddam's tyranny. However, it is a commonly held belief that the invasion had more to do with oil than with freeing people since there was no actual evidence of WMDs in Iraq or evidence that Saddam had any relationship with al-Qaeda. Some believe the US wanted to stabilize the global oil supply and make sure there would be no disruptions in oil coming out of Iraq. Others believe it was Bush's way of asserting American dominance over the world again after the terrorist attacks.

Whatever the real reason, American troops invaded Iraq in March 2003. Some troops from other allied countries also joined in the invasion. By April, most of Baghdad was under American control, and Saddam had gone into hiding. In December, he was captured by the US and convicted and executed three years later in December 2006 by the Iraqi High Tribunal.

However, this did not immediately end the war. Instead, Saddam's removal led to a power vacuum.

The war in Iraq, also called the Second Persian Gulf War, lasted until December 2011, when the US finally withdrew from Iraq after it was unable to negotiate an extension of its stay with the Iraqi government. In November 2011, the Senate voted to end the war, and on December 15th, the war came to a formal end.

Bush's Domestic Policies

While Bush and his administration were busy with the War on Terror, he also had to deal with numerous crises domestically.

The Great Recession

One of the biggest challenges facing Bush at home was the Great Recession. It was viewed as the worst economic crisis the country had seen since the Great Depression.

The recession was caused by three main things:

- The unstable housing market. In the early 2000s, the housing market was booming, and lenders were approving mortgages to poor creditors. Many of the loans defaulted, and the housing market plummeted.
- Bank crisis.

- Dramatic fall of the stock market, which wiped out a large chunk of wealth.

In response to the recession, the American Recovery and Reinvestment Act of 2009 was passed by Congress. The act put aside $800 billion to help with the economy's recovery. Another program called Troubled Asset Relief Program (TARP) also helped the economy grow. Bush also introduced tax relief that helped small businesses.

Health Care

When it came to America's health care, Bush helped to strengthen it by reforming Medicare and adding drug benefits. His policies gave approximately forty million people better access to prescription drugs. His reforms were aimed at making health care more affordable and accessible for Americans.

Bush won a second term as president, partially due to his heightened popularity immediately after 9/11 and his campaign against terrorism. His time in office was marked by a number of really difficult events, but as a president, he was fairly unremarkable.

The legacy he left behind is mainly tied to 9/11 and terrorism and his poor handling of Katrina. Ironically, he has become more respected and popular in his post-presidency years.

Hurricane Katrina

The fall of 2005 was a particularly difficult period in Bush's presidency. In addition to 9/11, which eventually led to the war in Iraq, President Bush also had to deal with the devastating consequences of Hurricane Katrina.

A Category 5 tropical cyclone, Katrina swept over The Bahamas and hit the southeastern United States on August 23rd, 2005. When it made landfall near the Miami and Fort Lauderdale area in Florida, it was a Category 1 hurricane, but over the following days, as it continued to move and circulate, it gained strength. When it finally arrived in New Orleans, it had turned into a Category 5. Southern Louisiana felt the brunt of the hurricane.

With 1,392 fatalities, Katrina would become one of the deadliest hurricanes. It would also become the most expensive hurricane to ever hit the country, causing between $97 and $145.5 billion in damages.

President Bush's response to Katrina was heavily criticized at the time and continues to be viewed in a negative manner to this day. His administration was slow to respond to the disaster and did not act decisively or empathetically. It took days for federal troops to make their way to the area. To make matters worse, while Katrina was pummeling the Gulf coast, Bush was on vacation in Texas and remained there. When he did return to Washington, he flew over New Orleans, viewing the devastation from above. The public perception of this move further damaged his image.

However, once Bush got the ball rolling, 7,200 troops were dispatched to New Orleans. On September 2nd, he signed a $10.5 billion relief package. Over the years, government assistance increased dramatically and is estimated to be somewhere between $126 billion and $140 billion, including tax reliefs. Bush also made sure to visit the area several times and meet with people.

However, the impression etched in people's minds was that he could have and should have done more.

Chapter 30: Barack Obama: The First Black President

During the 1950s and especially in the 1960s, when riots, violence, and protests around the civil rights movement were at their peak, it seemed unimaginable that, one day, America could have a black president.

In 2008, Barack Obama won the presidential election, becoming the forty-fourth president of America. He was the first African American president. It was a monumental and historic event. Suddenly, it felt as if nothing was impossible in America anymore.

President Obama.
https://commons.wikimedia.org/wiki/File:President_Barack_Obama.jpg

After the stressful, angst-filled years under the Bush administration, Obama felt like a fresh start, a hopeful beginning, and the turning of the tide to most of America.

Obama's Domestic Policies

During Obama's two terms as president, he contributed positively and negatively to the country. When he took office, he inherited an America that was going through many challenges. It was struggling to recover from an economic collapse and dealing with the aftermath of several wars, including the War on Terror. American troops were embroiled in a war in Afghanistan, and the future seemed bleak.

While campaigning, Obama promised the American people he would revive the economy, cut the deficit in half, and close the highly controversial US detention center in Guantanamo Bay in Cuba, where prisoners were rumored to be tortured and abused. He promised to bring about change and ensure America's stature globally. They were big promises to make. While Obama certainly left an enduring legacy and did a lot for the country, he wasn't able to keep all his promises.

During Obama's first term, he passed acts on three important issues: the economy, health care, and financial institutions.

One of his economic policies, the American Recovery and Reinvestment Act of 2009, helped to jumpstart the economy and decrease the unemployment rate. Tax reliefs provided a much-needed boost to American incomes and prevented approximately 5.3 million from slipping below the poverty line.

Obama helped restructure the American International Group (the country's largest insurer) to prevent future collapses. He did the same with the financial system to make sure institutions would be able to withstand any economic downturns. Obama's policies also brought stability to the housing crisis and saved the automotive industry.

His biggest legacy might be the signing of the Affordable Care Act. Obama pledged to make health care affordable and equal for all, as he believed that health care was a right and not a privilege. As we've seen in previous sections, health care had been a hotly contested issue during numerous presidencies. The act, commonly referred to as Obamacare, ensured that every American could afford a health insurance plan. The act mandates that all health insurance companies have to provide a certain type of coverage with their plans.

This was life-changing for struggling families that could not even afford to see a doctor. The most impacted families were blacks, minorities, small business owners, and those who fell below the poverty line.

Unfortunately, not everyone was a fan of the act. One of the main reasons people didn't support Obamacare has more to do with partisan politics than the act itself. Some Democrats felt the act didn't do enough and gave insurance companies too much control. They wanted to move toward a health care system that was fully run by the government.

On the other hand, many Republicans felt very strongly that the federal government should stay out of the health care system. They also opposed the tax increases that were necessary to get the act rolling, as well as the higher premiums with insurance companies.

The hike in premiums left some people feeling that health care was costing a lot more than it did in the past. This wasn't helped by the rising costs in health care and cost of living.

Obamacare did not provide the free, universal health care that some have dreamed of, but it was the start of something and changed the lives of millions of Americans.

Obama and the LGBTQ Community

According to LGBTQ advocates, President Obama was the most pro-LGBTQ president. He did a lot to advance their cause. Bush's administration had done nothing for the community; in fact, he set them back by supporting a constitutional amendment that would ban same-sex marriage.

Obama promised to do the opposite. He wanted his administration to work hard to support them. In 2009, the right to same-sex marriage was enshrined in the Constitution. Federal and state governments no longer had the authority to ban same-sex marriages.

A federal hate crime law was also passed that year to protect the rights of LGBTQ people. Clinton's "don't ask, don't tell" policy was repealed in 2010, allowing LGBTQ members of the military to serve without prejudice. In addition to these steps, Obama also signed executive orders to protect the LGBTQ community from being discriminated against by employers.

He was the first president to support marriage equality, as well as the first one to acknowledge the existence of transgender people, even inviting the executive director of the National Center for Transgender Equality to the White House.

Obama's actions advanced the LGBTQ community's progress by leaps and bounds after remaining stagnant for decades.

Domestic Crises

At home, several disastrous and tragic events unfolded during Obama's presidency, which required him to rally the country and provide emotional support and strength.

One such tragedy was the Sandy Hook Elementary school shooting, which took place on December 14th, 2012. It was the deadliest elementary school shooting in American history, leaving twenty children and six adults dead. The shooter was twenty-year-old Adam Lanza.

After killing his own mother in their home with a rifle she had purchased for him, he gathered his other weapons and drove to the elementary school. He gained entrance into the locked school by shooting a window around 9:30 in the morning. His rampage lasted for less than eleven minutes and ended with him taking his own life.

Later that day, Obama addressed the American public and said tragedies like this had to be brought to an end and that change was necessary. Despite his desire to change gun control laws, by the time he left office, very little progress had been made.

Another notable tragedy was the Boston Marathon bombings. This terrorist attack was perpetrated by two brothers who were Chechen Kyrgyzstani Americans.

While the Boston Marathon was taking place on April 15th, 2013, the two brothers detonated two bombs close to the race's finish line. Three people died, and hundreds of other people were injured, many of whom lost body parts and became permanently disabled.

Obama once again spoke to the American people and paid tribute to the victims and everyone else involved with the rescue efforts. In each of these incidents, he grieved with the nation and comforted the people, much like Bill Clinton had done after the Columbine massacre.

Obama's Foreign Policies

Aside from an economic mess, Obama also inherited two wars in Iraq and Afghanistan that Bush had started during his campaign against terror. One of his campaign promises was that he would withdraw American troops from the wars and establish better relations.

A year into his first term, Obama announced that the number of American troops serving overseas would be scaled down drastically from 160,000 troops to 50,000 within the year. He planned for the rest to be withdrawn by 2011. The process went as planned, and by 2012, there were only 150 American troops still stationed in Iraq.

However, in Afghanistan, Obama agreed to the military's request to send an additional twenty-one thousand troops into the country to keep the Taliban regime in check. He soon decided that a new course of action would be required in Afghanistan since the war had been dragging on for so long. He felt the Afghanistan government needed to be in a position to defeat the Taliban on its own.

One of his greatest achievements in the fight against the Taliban regime was the killing of Osama bin Laden, the leader of al-Qaeda and the mastermind behind 9/11. Navy SEALS killed him in May 2011. American soldiers began to disengage from the region in earnest after this.

Obama also managed to restore America's diplomatic ties with Cuba, which had been severed since the early days of the Cold War.

Obama and ISIS

When ISIS grew in power, Obama, at first, underestimated the threat. Knowing that Americans and the government were feeling "war-weary," he wanted to change the narrative of America perpetually fighting in wars. So, he chose not to launch strikes in Syria or do anything to stop the rebel group. Unchecked, the radicals expanded dramatically into a dangerous, extremist group.

In 2014, Obama spoke to the Americans and stated he would destroy ISIS. Within weeks, he ordered strikes on ISIS targets in

Syria. The number of American troops in Iraq was increased to help fight against ISIS. By the time his tenure as president ended, the situation in Iraq and Syria remained unstable and precarious.

Adding to an already complicated situation, Russian leader Vladimir Putin had growing ambitions in the Middle East and Ukraine, where he ordered a military occupation. Sanctions from America and other countries did nothing to change his plans.

Obama's Wars

As a direct or indirect consequence of America's war against ISIS, the Taliban, and al-Qaeda, the US ended up getting involved in a number of other wars. Obama's campaign promise to end American involvement in grueling international conflicts like Iraq and Afghanistan was one he was unable to keep. Obama won the Nobel Peace Prize in 2009 but publicly stated that he felt certain events and circumstances justified a country going to war.

For the entirety of his presidency, American forces remained at war, with military campaigns in at least seven countries: Iraq, Syria, Afghanistan, Libya, Pakistan, Somalia, and Yemen.

Why did he begin these wars? The causes are varied and complicated, but here is a quick breakdown.

- The involvement in Iraq began with humanitarian crises that could have impacted American interests and quickly evolved into a fight against ISIS.
- At first, Obama tried to stay out of Syria, even when Syrian President Bashar al-Assad authorized the use of chemical weapons against the civilian population. However, when ISIS became a serious and viable threat, Obama felt he had no choice but to attack the country.
- Afghanistan was an inherited war that Obama started to put an end to by withdrawing troops when a new president came to power in the country.
- The war in Libya began as part of a UN mission with allied powers to protect Libyan civilians from an oppressive regime. The UN Security Council approved the use of force. After Moammar Gadhafi's death, the air strikes in Libya stopped. However, the situation in Libya is anything

but stable today.

- America got involved in Pakistan because of the Taliban.
- Somalia was attacked due to its affiliations with a terrorist network.
- Yemen faced threats from al-Qaeda.

In each situation, Obama felt he had to intervene for American security and interests. However, it doesn't change the fact that when he left office, the country was involved in more wars than when he came in.

One of the crucial things that changed was the way war was fought. Obama moved away from traditional troops battling it out in war zones, preferring to use elite commando units and technology like cyber weapons and armed drones. Obama authorized nearly 550 drone strikes, which killed nearly 4,000 people. Some of these were civilian deaths.

Obama's Legacy

The impact of Obama's legacy and his popularity with the American people cannot be denied. He had his critics. Many people did not agree with his style of governing. He had an average approval rating of 47.9 percent, and when he left office, he did so with an approval rating of 53 percent, just slightly below that of two other enormously popular presidents, Reagan and Clinton.

Obama tried to fix many of the challenges America was facing in the early 2000s and did a lot of good. Unfortunately, he also embroiled America in more international conflicts.

However, the biggest and most enduring legacy he left behind was that a black man of humble origins and a middle-class upbringing could become president. Suddenly, it didn't seem all that impossible to imagine a woman or a minority becoming president. His legacy is one of hope that anything *can* be possible.

Chapter 31: Donald Trump: A Controversial President

As Obama's presidency ended, so did any semblance of normality for America and the world at large. Donald Trump's astonishing win in the 2016 presidential election disrupted the world order and ushered in a period of turbulence and deep instability, both at home and abroad.

But first, let's take a quick look at Trump and how he became the forty-fifth president of the United States.

Donald Trump

Born in a wealthy family to parents of German descent, Trump attended private schools and had a privileged upbringing. He eventually joined his father's business called Trump Management. In the early 1970s, he was made president of the company.

Trump soon renamed the business to Trump Organization and expanded into real estate. Over the years, he created a billion-dollar empire and went on to dabble in a number of different things, including having his own television show, *The Apprentice*.

He also dabbled in different political parties. He was a Republican in 1987. A decade later, he was affiliated with the Reform Party. A few years later, in 2001, he was registered as a Democrat before switching back to Republican in 2009.

On June 16th, 2015, Trump held a campaign rally in New York City at Trump Tower. He came down a golden escalator and announced his intention to run for president. Trump ran against Democratic candidate Hillary Clinton, whose educational background, time in Washington, and accomplishments showed that she was a suitable candidate to run the country. Trump, on the other hand, captivated the people, although he had no real political background, instead focusing on running a business empire.

In a stunning turn of events, Trump won the election.

President Donald Trump.
Gage Skidmore; This file is licensed under the Creative Commons Attribution-Share Alike 2.0 Generic license; https://en.wikipedia.org/wiki/File:Donald_Trump_%28300230826449%29.jpg

How did Trump do it?

He echoed the message of Ronald Reagan by promising to "make America great again." This simple message meant something to a significant portion of the population. Tired of the wars and tired of feeling that nothing was being done for their country, many people liked the message of the nation becoming great once more and regaining what had been lost.

While Hillary appealed to people's logic, providing cool, thoughtful proposals and promises, Trump appealed to people's emotions. It didn't matter that his promises made no sense or were illogical; he said what people wanted to hear.

Another thing Trump had on his side was the fear of electing a woman as president. A woman had never led the country before, and it seemed many Americans were not prepared for that. Many people (women included) also harbored an intense dislike for Hillary as the woman who supported her husband during his sex scandal. Some viewed her as controlling and "bossy." The email scandal from her time as secretary of state during Obama's presidency also resurfaced and was detrimental to her campaign. The scandal had to do with Hillary using her private email server to handle sensitive and classified information. It led to an FBI probe and investigation. Even though Hillary publicly apologized and took accountability for it, the scandal played a huge role in why people didn't trust her. The FBI eventually determined that none of the documents were marked classified.

Whatever the reasons may be, Trump won the election. Hillary won the popular vote. She had almost three million more votes than Trump, making her loss the largest popular vote margin in US history.

America First

Trump talked a lot about putting "America First," but what did that mean?

The concept of America First wasn't a new one; it dated back to a Republican campaign slogan that was first used as early as the 1880s. It was the notion that American nationalism should come first and that the country should maintain a non-interventionist stance.

Trump's America First policies were highly controversial because it was a complete break from the role the United States had played for many decades. After the end of the two world wars, America emerged as a superpower. The nation often played a peacekeeper role and worked to maintain balance in the international order. America was seen as a diverse, multicultural, democratic nation where human rights, equality, and individual freedoms were prioritized.

Previous presidents strongly felt that America had a moral duty to fulfill a certain role. Trump's stance shifted dramatically away from this. He also unleashed some thoughts and beliefs that many had kept in check for years, with his values giving rise to the notion of white supremacy.

Some key points of the Trump administration's economic policies include the following:

- Tax cuts for individuals and corporations
- Efforts to get rid of and replace Obama's Affordable Care Act
- Restrictions on immigration

His policies had a direct impact on numerous acts and agreements. Let's take a brief look at some notable events and moments from Trump's presidency.

Immigration Policies

For decades, America had been a country where new immigrants flocked to in droves, mostly in search of a better life and the "American Dream."

One of Trump's immediate priorities was to crack down on immigration. He famously talked about erecting a wall between Mexico and the United States to prevent migrants from illegally crossing over.

Some of the things he implemented as part of his immigration policies include the following:

- Phasing out the Deferred Action for Childhood Arrivals (DACA). The name DREAMers (for the Development, Relief, and Education for Alien Minors Act) was given to children who entered the country through illegal means as a child. Under DACA, they did not have the same rights as an American citizen (for instance, they could not vote), but they were allowed to work, have a social security number, and many other things. Trump tried to dismantle the program on numerous occasions. DACA was approved to continue with some minor changes in August 2022.
- Separating family members at the Mexico border. Children were taken away from their parents or guardians. While the adults were prosecuted legally, the children were taken away and put in holding centers. Many families will likely never again be reunited.

- Imposing a travel ban and suspending the arrival of refugees

These are just some of the policies he implemented, essentially ripping apart everything that America has stood for, especially in the eyes of other countries around the world.

Dissolution of NAFTA and the New USMCA Agreement

Trump dissolved NAFTA with Mexico and Canada, which had been in effect since 1994. The agreement allowed for free trade between the three countries and increased trading between them. Every day, approximately $1.4 billion of goods flowed across the border.

In Trump's views, NAFTA was one of the worst deals the US had ever made, and he made it clear during the elections that he was going to get rid of it if he was elected. While it's true NAFTA resulted in the loss of about 800,000 jobs over nearly two decades, over 6 million jobs were dependent on continued trade with Mexico. It also kept the cost of goods low for consumers.

Trump repealed the agreement and replaced it with USMCA (United States-Mexico-Canada Agreement) in 2018. Essentially, the new document was just an update of the old agreement. According to Trump, the updates should create 176,000 new jobs by 2024. It is not yet clear whether the United States is on track to meet this goal.

When Obama became president, an important foreign policy goal for him was to maintain peace and foster a better relationship with Cuba. He did so by removing Cuba from the list of blacklisted countries. Trump's approach to foreign policy has been focused mostly on America first, and as such, he reversed Obama's decision in early 2021. His administration imposed new sanctions on Cuba and redesignated the country as a "state sponsor of terrorism," which includes other countries like North Korea, Syria, and Iran.

Trade with China

Trump was determined to crack down on trade negotiations with China, but this agreement was more unclear. The agreement signed in January 2018 left many things unresolved.

When Trump imposed trade tariffs on China, he was trying to force the country to change what he believed was unfair trading and lower the trade deficit it had with America.

In 2021, a study was conducted to see whether Trump's trade war with China was profitable. Instead of being profitable, his impulsive trade policies cost the American economy around one-quarter million jobs.

Paris Climate Agreement

On December 12th, 2015, 196 countries agreed to an international treaty around climate change called the Paris Agreement. Under the treaty, the participating countries agreed to reduce their greenhouse gas emissions to limit global warming and achieve climate neutrality. This was a landmark treaty because, for the first time in history, most of the world was working together toward a common goal: to combat climate change.

Within a year of taking office, Trump announced his intention to withdraw from the Paris Climate Agreement. Delays with UN regulations meant there was a three-year delay. By the time the withdrawal took effect, a new presidential election was underway.

In 2021, after Biden was elected president, the US rejoined the Paris Climate Agreement.

Abraham Accords

Nearly every president has had a say in the ongoing conflict in the Middle East, and Trump was no different. One of his most notable achievements was the Abraham Accords.

The Abraham Accords was an agreement reached between the United States, the United Arab Emirates, Bahrain, and Israel on August 13th, 2020, to improve the relationship between the countries. It was named Abraham since he is a prophet in both Judaism and Islam. Morocco and Sudan later signed the accords as well.

As the Palestine-Israel conflict continues to escalate, Biden is trying to use the accords to encourage other Arab countries to also normalize their relationships with Israel.

Coronavirus Pandemic

The latter part of Trump's presidency came to a halt as a pandemic swept through the world. The Trump administration was woefully unprepared for the virus, as Trump had disbanded the pandemic response team in 2018.

Utter chaos and confusion followed, with Trump refusing to acknowledge that there was even an issue. He even praised China for handling the virus in an effective manner and assured the American people that the pandemic would not touch them or enter the country, even as he was being advised to the contrary by experts.

Some of Trump's claims during the crisis included denying the virus, saying it would miraculously go away in the spring, that it was nothing more than the flu, that claims of deaths were grossly exaggerated, and that none of this was his fault.

Trump did pass bills that helped Americans with their daily living needs. However, most still believe that Trump did not handle the pandemic in a suitable manner, with detractors saying his administration left Americans to fend for themselves.

Presidential Election of 2020

When the 2020 presidential election rolled around, Trump announced his intention to seek reelection. A significant majority of Americans and the world felt strongly a second term under Trump would be disastrous, yet it seemed quite likely that he would win another term.

Joe Biden, Obama's vice president, who had previously said he would never run for president, became the presidential nominee for the Democratic Party.

An intense period of campaigning followed between the two nominees, and on November 3rd, 2020, Biden won the election. Trump refused to concede defeat and claimed voter fraud had taken place and that he had, in fact, won the election.

He and his supporters continued to spread these ideas, and on January 6th, 2021, when the election results were being certified in the Capitol, Trump supporters attacked the Capitol. The mob was determined to interfere in the transfer of power and claim the presidency for Trump. As rioters stormed toward the Capitol, Trump did nothing to stop them immediately. As of this writing, the Justice Department is winding down its official investigation into Trump's role in the riot.

Despite the rioting, the certification was completed. Joe Biden was officially recognized as president-elect. He was inaugurated on

January 20th, 2021, as the forty-sixth president. Since taking office, he has worked hard to overturn many of Trump's policies and reforms. He also prioritized the pandemic by signing a $1.9 trillion relief bill and promised Americans a quick rollout of vaccines. By his 100th day in office, the Biden administration had managed to deliver 200 million vaccines.

Many of Biden's campaign promises centered around bringing America and the presidency back to what it was before Trump. Whether or not that can be managed remains to be seen, as some of Trump's policies have changed the landscape of America, and their effects will last for decades to come.

For instance, Trump nominated three Supreme Court judges (an unheard-of feat) in the modern day. This changed the balance of power in the Supreme Court, which meant many important court rulings could be more easily overturned. This happened on June 24th, 2022, when the Supreme Court overturned Roe v. Wade, a landmark legislation that had made the right and access to abortion a federal right.

The true cost of these decisions will likely be seen and felt in the decades to come.

Conclusion: Looking Forward

The United States is a remarkable nation that was built and created out of almost nothing. A group of people with a dream got together centuries ago and decided they wanted to cut ties with Europe and forge their own paths. And through all of the country's ups and downs, this is the theme that endures: the desire to be independent, to be a leader, and to follow a dream.

Dreams of equality spurred women's movements and civil rights movements. The pursuit of the American dream brings thousands of new immigrants into the country to this day.

There is no doubt the last few years have been turbulent ones for America, both at home and internationally. But this is nothing they haven't lived through before. If we can learn anything from America's history, it's that the United States always finds a way of overcoming the odds and coming out on top.

As the world begins to settle into a new post-pandemic reality under the guidance of a new administration, the hope is that America will once more regain the prestige and influence it used to enjoy and be a beacon of democracy, human rights, and equality.

Here's another book by Enthralling History that you might like

Free limited time bonus

Stop for a moment. We have a free bonus set up for you. The problem is this: we forget 90% of everything that we read after 7 days. Crazy fact, right? Here's the solution: we've created a printable, 1-page pdf summary for this book that you're reading now. All you have to do to get your free pdf summary is to go to the following website: **https://livetolearn.lpages.co/enthrallinghistory/**

Once you do, it will be intuitive. Enjoy, and thank you!

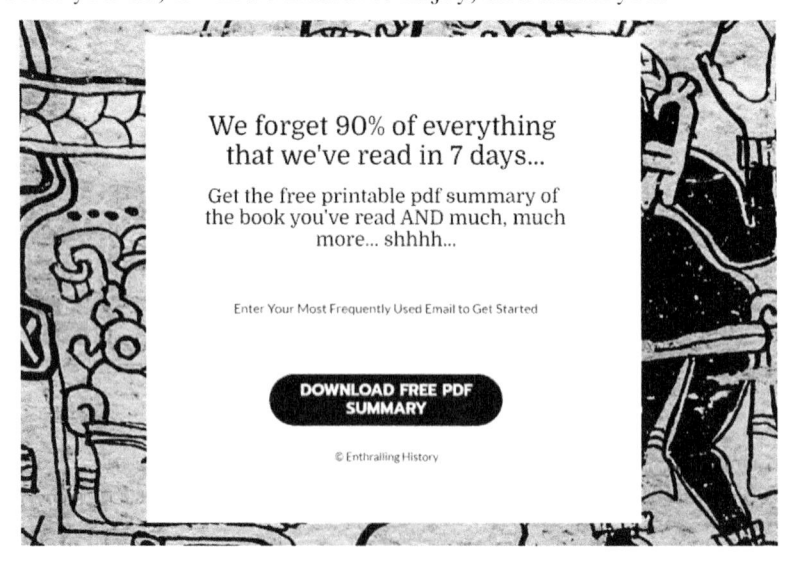

Sources

https://www.history.com/topics/exploration/francisco-vazquez-de-coronado

https://www.history.com/topics/colonial-america/thirteen-colonies

https://www.history.com/this-day-in-history/new-amsterdam-becomes-new-york#:~:text=Following%20its%20capture%2C%20New%20Amsterdam%27s,Island%2C%20Connecticut%20and%20New%20Jersey.

https://www.britannica.com/event/American-Revolution

https://www.history.com/news/american-revolution-causes

https://www.loc.gov/classroom-materials/united-states-history-primary-source-timeline/american-revolution-1763-1783/british-reforms-1763-1766/

https://www.nps.gov/subjects/americanrevolution/timeline.htm

https://www.worldatlas.com/articles/major-battles-of-the-american-revolutionary-war.html

https://www.battlefields.org/learn/articles/10-facts-founding-fathers#:~:text=Fact%20%231%3A%20These%20seven%20men,John%20Jay%20and%20James%20Madison.

https://www.whitehouse.gov/about-the-white-house/our-government/the-constitution/

https://history.state.gov/milestones/1776-1783/articles

https://www.mtsu.edu/first-amendment/article/1118/bill-of-rights#:~:text=To%20ensure%20ratification%20of%20the,fourths%20of%20the%20state%20legislatures.

https://www.usa.gov/branches-of-government#item-214500

https://www.history.com/topics/us-presidents/george-washington#americas-first-president

https://www.britannica.com/event/Louisiana-Purchase

https://www.history.com/topics/war-of-1812/war-of-1812

https://www.digitalhistory.uh.edu/disp_textbook.cfm?smtID=2&psid=2986

https://www.battlefields.org/learn/war-1812/battles/tippecanoe

https://www.semtribe.com/stof/history/seminoles-today

https://www.history.com/topics/native-american-history/trail-of-tears

https://www.thecanadianencyclopedia.ca/en/article/northwest-territories-and-confederation

https://www.encyclopedia.com/history/dictionaries-thesauruses-pictures-and-press-releases/oregon-treaty-1846

https://history.state.gov/milestones/1830-1860/texas-annexation

https://www.nps.gov/civilwar/facts.htm#:~:text=The%20Union%20included%20the%20states,Abraham%20Lincoln%20was%20their%20President.

https://www.history.com/topics/american-civil-war/vicksburg-campaign

https://www.nps.gov/articles/a-short-overview-of-the-battle-of-antietam.htm

https://www.historynet.com/battle-of-fredericksburg/

https://www.history.com/news/7-things-you-should-know-about-the-battle-of-gettysburg

https://www.ducksters.com/history/civil_war/border_states.php

https://www.archives.gov/publications/prologue/2010/spring/newnation.html

https://www.pbs.org/wgbh/americanexperience/features/grant-impeachment/

https://learn.uakron.edu/beyond/industrialage.htm

https://guides.loc.gov/chronicling-america-spanish-american-war

https://www.ushistory.org/us/44b.asp

https://www.khanacademy.org/humanities/us-history/rise-to-world-power/age-of-empire/a/the-progressive-era#:~:text=The%20period%20of%20US%20history,progress%20toward%20a%20better%20society.

https://www.smithsonianmag.com/history/when-roosevelt-and-jp-morgan-fixed-coal-mine-strike-180975311/

https://www.history.com/news/the-strike-that-shook-america

https://www.pbs.org/tpt/slavery-by-another-name/themes/progressivism/

https://www.khanacademy.org/humanities/us-history/the-gilded-age/american-west/a/the-dawes-act

https://www.loc.gov/classroom-materials/immigration/native-american/removing-native-americans-from-their-land/

https://www.mnhs.org/fortsnelling/learn/us-dakota-war#:~:text=The%20Fort%20Snelling%20Concentration%20Camp&text=In%20December%20soldiers%20built%20a,a%20hospital%20and%20mission%20station.

https://www.historytoday.com/archive/months-past/end-great-sioux-war

https://www.legendsofamerica.com/warren-wagon-train-raid/

https://www.doi.gov/blog/conservation-legacy-theodore-roosevelt#:~:text=After%20becoming%20president%20in%201901,is%20found%20across%20the%20country.

https://www.pbs.org/wgbh/americanexperience/features/carnegie-biography/

https://www.khanacademy.org/humanities/us-history/rise-to-world-power/us-in-wwi/a/the-league-of-nations#:~:text=The%20League%20of%20Nations%20was,opposition%20from%20isolationists%20in%20Congress.

https://www.history.com/topics/roaring-twenties/roaring-twenties-history

https://www.history.com/this-day-in-history/truman-doctrine-is-announced

https://www.history.com/topics/world-war-ii/marshall-plan-1

https://www.khanacademy.org/humanities/us-history/postwarera/postwar-era/a/start-of-the-cold-war-part-2

https://en.wikipedia.org/wiki/Third_World#Development_aid

https://www.history.com/topics/black-history/martin-luther-king-jr-assassination#king-assassination-conspiracy

https://www.jfklibrary.org/learn/education/teachers/curricular-resources/elementary-school-curricular-resources/ask-not-what-your-country-can-do-for-you

https://study.com/academy/lesson/culture-of-1960s-america.html

https://www.history.com/news/vietnam-war-origins-events

https://www.britannica.com/topic/oil-crisis

https://www.worldbank.org/en/about/history/the-world-bank-group-and-the-imf

https://www.history.com/this-day-in-history/helsinki-final-act-signed

https://www.history.com/news/jimmy-carter-camp-david-accords-egypt-israel

https://en.wikipedia.org/wiki/1979_oil_crisis#Effects
https://www.studysmarter.us/explanations/history/cold-war/second-cold-war/
https://www.american-historama.org/1945-1989-cold-war-era/iran-contra-affair.htm
https://www.history.com/topics/1980s/iran-contra-affair
https://www.encyclopedia.com/history/encyclopedias-almanacs-transcripts-and-maps/malta-summit
https://www.nps.gov/articles/start-treaty-1991.htm
https://history.state.gov/departmenthistory/short-history/firstgulf
https://www.britannica.com/event/Persian-Gulf-War
https://millercenter.org/president/clinton/domestic-affairs
https://srebrenica.org.uk/what-happened/bosnian-war-a-brief-overview
https://time.com/5120561/bill-clinton-monica-lewinsky-timeline/
https://www.pbs.org/wgbh/pages/frontline/shows/kosovo/etc/cron.html
https://www.georgewbushlibrary.gov/research/topic-guides/global-war-terror
https://www.history.com/this-day-in-history/baghdad-falls-iraq-war
https://www.acorns.com/learn/investing/what-caused-great-recession-of-2008/
https://obamawhitehouse.archives.gov/the-record/economy
https://www.cms.gov/Regulations-and-Guidance/Legislation/Recovery
https://millercenter.org/president/obama/foreign-affairs
https://www.cnn.com/2014/09/23/politics/countries-obama-bombed/index.html
https://www.vox.com/policy-and-politics/2017/1/17/14214522/obama-lgbtq-legacy
https://en.wikipedia.org/wiki/Paris_Agreement
https://doggett.house.gov/media/blog-post/timeline-trumps-coronavirus-responses
https://www.cnn.com/2021/04/28/politics/president-biden-first-100-days/index.html

Printed in Dunstable, United Kingdom